CECILE ROSSANT

Underground New York

CORNELSEN ENGLISH LIBRARY

Cornelsen

Cornelsen English Library
Cecile Rossant

Verlagsredaktion
Stefan Höhne, Christiane Kallenbach

Umschlaggestaltung
hawemannundmosch, Konzeption und Gestaltung, Berlin

Bildquellen
Umschlag: **Steve Duncane** / Undercity.org
Alamy, Abingdon (S. 12: Kris Legg (RF)); **Corbis**, Düsseldorf (S. 13: Bettmann/ Lewis Wickes Hine); **Larkin Dugan**, New York (S. 22); **David Morrow**, New York (S. 58, S. 79, S. 88, S. 90 , S. 91, S. 110); **ullstein bild**, Berlin (S. 72: ullstein bild, S. 122: Granger Collection); **Timothy Vogel**, New York (S. 41, S. 127)

Gestaltung & technische Umsetzung
Ilona und Ingo Ostermaier, Fredersdorf

www.cornelsen.de
www.EnglishG.de

Dieses Werk folgt der amerikanischen Rechtschreibung.

1. Auflage, 9. Druck 2021

Alle Drucke dieser Auflage sind inhaltlich unverändert
und können im Unterricht nebeneinander verwendet werden.

Druck: H. Heenemann, Berlin

ISBN 978-3-06-032302-9

PEFC
PEFC/04-31-1156

PEFC zertifiziert
Dieses Produkt stammt aus nachhaltig bewirtschafteten Wäldern und kontrollierten Quellen.

www.pefc.de

Contents

Chapter 1

Zoe Kranbacher pressed her face to the glass that separated the baggage claim area from the arrivals gate, while Basti Kranbacher, her older brother, waited for their suitcases at the other end of the large airport hall. Through the glass, she saw a teenage boy standing behind the ropes. He was wearing baggy jeans, an old red T-shirt and high top basketball shoes. Could that be Rick? It must be him! But he looks different, she thought. This boy was much taller than her cousin and had a mustache or a strange shadow above his mouth that was even darker than Basti's. There was something else that didn't fit – his hair! Rick had light brown hair, but the boy's was black, very black. She knocked on the glass to catch his attention, but he didn't see her. It must be very noisy out there, she thought. A very tall man in khaki shorts and sandals and a girl Zoe's age then walked up to the boy – Uncle Ben and Debbie! So that was Rick. Wow, he had changed. Zoe knocked again. They seemed to be looking in her direction but still they didn't see her.

Zoe had last seen her cousins two years ago when the whole family came to Germany for the summer vacation. They had traveled to the seaside together and had had a great time – except for when Basti and Rick had buried her up to her shoulders in the sand and then ran away. Zoe had to wait until Debbie helped her out. That wasn't fun. It was just plain mean! Uncle Ben was her mother's younger brother. He was always making jokes and loved sports – almost the opposite of her father. What did dad say the night before they left for New York? He just held her close and said, I'm going to miss both of you. And then, holding her face in his hands, he said very seriously, "Be careful, Zoe, New York is a big city and every big city can be dangerous. That's what makes it exciting. But you have to keep your eyes open and always ask yourself if you're walking into something you really know too little about. Remember, ask questions and always let Uncle Ben and Aunt Marion know where you're going. Got that? Just in case something goes wrong they've got to know where you are, OK?" Yes, that's what he said: New York can be a dangerous place. Was New York more dangerous than Frankfurt, Berlin or Munich? she wondered.

Zoe banged on the glass once more and, still unable to get their attention, she decided she'd better go back and help Basti.

Meanwhile, Basti was sleepily staring at the suitcases, boxes and baby carriages that passed by him. It was all the baggage from flight number 689, non-stop from Frankfurt to John F Kennedy Airport, New York. Where is she? he thought. She's always disappearing. It was true. Zoe was always wandering away. From the age of three she was already exploring the world beyond the playground – following birds and butterflies, a boy on a red plastic car, an old man in a wheelchair, a flying plastic bag or a bright green balloon.

Basti took his eyes off the suitcases and nervously looked across the large hall for his sister. There was no sign of her. The night before they left for New York dad had told him and Zoe never to lose sight of each other. He had looked at Basti and then back at Zoe. Dad had meant these last words for him – that was clear. The big message was that he had the top responsibility on this trip. Of course, he was the older one.

"Ich hab sie gesehen!" shouted Zoe as she ran towards Basti. A camera hanging from her neck by a bright red strap bounced from side to side as she flew across the hall. She looks funny, Basti thought. Zoe's brown hair was mussed up from sleeping on the plane. She was wearing an 'I ❤ NY' T-shirt and jean shorts. With her new digital camera she looked like a typical tourist.

Zoe stopped, excited, when she reached him.

"Hey, we're in New York now. Time to start speaking English," Basti said in a teacherly voice.

"Yeah, OK. *Ich hab Onkel … ich meine … ich bin zu aufgeregt, ich kann jetzt kein Englisch sprechen!"* said Zoe throwing her arms up into the air. *"Ich hab Onkel Ben, Rick und Debbie gesehen, durch das Fenster … da!"* Before Basti could react, Zoe jumped towards the luggage carousel. She had spotted Basti's old brown suitcase and tried to pull it off. It was too heavy. From behind, a man's hand grabbed the side strap and together he and Zoe pulled the suitcase off the moving black track.

"Thank you!" she said. There. Her first English sentence.

"Kein Problem," answered the man with a smile. Of course, she thought, he just came from Frankfurt, and speaks German just like we do.

"There's mine!" said Zoe pointing to a green suitcase covered with stickers from every place she had ever visited. This time she let Basti pull it off.

With their four hands pushing the baggage cart, they raced through customs and the "Nothing to declare" area and through the automatic doors.

"There they are!" said Debbie, hitting her father on the arm.

"Hi guys," said Rick cooly. "Let me take your bags."

Debbie looked around embarrassedly but then ran up and hugged Zoe and then Basti.

"Welcome to New York!" said Uncle Ben in a booming voice.

Zoe took a step back from her uncle's warm embrace to have a better look at Debbie. It always took a while to really see her. Debbie was shy – the quiet type. She was now too old to hide behind her mother or father's legs but still she always seemed to be in the background. Her soft-looking, reddish-blond hair fell in front of her face and she was very thin. She reminded Zoe of a baby giraffe.

With Rick it was a very different story. He was cool and funny. There was something going on his head, you could see it. Plans, music, and something secret. And now he even wore an earring in his left ear.

It was the middle of July, and as soon as they left the air-conditioned building something hit Zoe in the face. It was the hot air. It felt as if she had walked right into a sauna.

"Wow, is it hot out here!" she said.

"Welcome to the famous New York City summer," said Uncle Ben. "New Yorkers call this weather 'muggy'."

"Muggy?" asked Basti, wanting to check if he was getting the pronunciation right.

"Yup, it means the same thing as *schwül* in German," said Uncle Ben with a smile. "When I first came here 22 years ago this weather killed me."

Basti and Zoe nodded, trying to get used to this strange weather and language.

It was so hot! But as soon as they got outside Zoe just had to run around and take pictures – of people's faces, of the green and white signs, and the overhead highway. This was her first trip to the US and she wanted to know about everything that was different here.

"This way, everybody. The car is over here," said Rick, pointing to an old Volvo.

"Which one of you will sit up front with me?" asked Uncle Ben.

"I'd like to," said Zoe.

"OK, then let Basti sit on the right," said Uncle Ben to Rick and Debbie, "so he can get the best view."

Once they were on the highway, the air-conditioner pleasantly humming, Uncle Ben asked about the family and school and explained that he and Marion, his wife, would be working during the week.

"But don't worry, Debbie and Rick will be your guides," he said reassuringly, "they know the city as well as I do. There's a lot to see."

They drove on in silence. After about twenty minutes on the road, Uncle Ben caught Basti's eye through the mirror. "OK, Basti and Zoe, keep your eyes open. If you look to our right, you'll get a great view of the Manhattan skyline."

Zoe pressed her face against the window. There it was: Manhattan. She had seen photos before. Her parents had a book with fancy pictures of all the skyscrapers and the skyline of Manhattan. But the real thing actually seemed more like a fantasy. The sky was clear, a deep blue tinged with orange around the buildings. Her watch read 2:00 pm. The sunlight was still strong, which made the buildings' shadows long and clear. There were so many towers: building after building, and all of them were packed so closely together. The skyline reminded her of the inside of a kitchen cupboard after her mom had gone food shopping. The cupboard was then so full with boxes, cans and bottles of all different sizes. Although you might just want to pick out a long package of butter cookies, you couldn't help but see the whole thing – the whole city in the cupboard.

Uncle Ben turned the car onto a ramp that led to a bridge. "We'll be crossing the East River from Brooklyn to Manhattan. On the Manhattan Bridge, if you look to your left, you can see the Brooklyn Bridge. It's pretty close to our house, but it's best on foot or by bike."

☆

"That's our building," said Uncle Ben, pointing to a 16-story tower. We're up on the 14th floor." Zoe and Basti tried to imagine what it would be like 14 floors up. Uncle Ben parked on a quiet street behind the building. He and Rick brought their suitcases to the entry. A man in a blue uniform and blue cap opened the door for them.

"Hi, George, how's it going?" said Uncle Ben.

"Afternoon, Mr. Meyer," said the man with a quick nod and reached for one of the bags.

"Let me help you with those," he said. Uncle Ben swung the bag away.

"I have to do something to stay fit, George! But let me introduce you to Rick and Debbie's cousins: Zoe and Sebastian. They've just arrived from Germany. They'll be staying with us for the next two weeks." Zoe and Sebastian walked up to shake hands with the man in uniform.

"*Irgendwie peinlich* ... This isn't a hotel. Why is this guy in a uniform here?" thought Zoe. She took a quick look around the lobby. It had peach-colored walls, brown tiles on the floor and behind Mr. George's desk, the wall was covered with mailboxes.

Uncle Ben led them to the elevator. Zoe was as excited as she was tired and hungry. Going up was a strange feeling. She saw herself in the mirror that covered one side of the elevator. She was surprised at how funny her hair looked and tried to smooth it down. She lifted her camera and looked at everybody in the mirror through her camera's eye.

"Can all of you look this way?" she asked, pointing to the mirror with her free hand. "I want to take a group photo." Looking through the viewfinder, she also saw her own face with a camera. She liked herself better that way: a self-portrait with camera.

"Do you ever walk up?" asked Basti.

"Just when the elevators are under repair. What do you say, Ricky? Happens at least once a month, right?" said Uncle Ben, patting his son on the back. He explained that there is always a doorman until 2 in the morning. After that the front door is locked. It's so strange, thought Zoe again, it's just like a hotel.

Rick and Debbie's mom, Aunt Marion, met them at the door. She gave each a warm squeeze. Zoe breathed in the smell of her nice perfume.

"You both must be tired after all that flying," said Marion, looking at her watch. "It's already 10 in the evening for you guys. Are you hungry?" she asked.

Zoe shrugged her shoulders. She was actually pretty hungry. It was over five hours ago since she had eaten. And even that hadn't been much. The meat in the little aluminum dish had tasted like warm shoes.

"No, not at all, we're fine," said Basti, who had eaten both her dinner as well as his own. And he had only given her his small bread roll in exchange!

"Well, then, come on in! Just drop your things and let me show you around." She led them into a bright living room with a view of the Hudson River.

"Wow!" said Zoe and Basti at the same time.

"We also have a balcony on this side. It's great in the summertime, but it's actually too windy to sit comfortably later in the year and too cold in winter. Come on, let me show you." Basti and Zoe followed her through the glass door onto a small balcony with a little green metal table and two chairs. There were potted plants in every corner. Basti looked down. Below there were people on in-line skates, kids riding bikes, babies on their dads' shoulders. Zoe saw bridges, a park and small and large boats crossing the river.

"That's New Jersey across the river, and if you look this way, you can see the Statue of Liberty. The island is south of here – or what we call 'Downtown'." Aunt Marion then pointed in the other direction. "This way is of course north, which New Yorkers call 'Uptown'."

"Ricky and Debbie!" Aunt Marion called out, tucking her head back into the living room. "Come and show Basti and Zoe where they'll be sleeping and where the bathroom is."

Rick led Basti down a corridor to his room and Debbie brought Zoe to her very neat room. The walls were painted the same peach color as the lobby and the room smelled like fruit-scented shampoo with a faint touch of bubble gum. Posters of Avril Lavigne and Rihanna as well as other pop stars Zoe didn't know were carefully pinned to the walls. There wasn't much floor space in the room with a second bed set up, so Zoe made a mental note not to make a mess of

Debbie's room. She would have to be a lot neater than she usually was at home. Debbie was showing her the wardrobe where she could put her clothes when Debbie's cellphone started playing a tune. Debbie answered and mimed "I'm sorry" by lifting her eyebrows. Zoe didn't feel like listening in. Rick's door was shut so she went back to the living room.

Her eyes were caught by two framed photographs. The first showed a thin spiral staircase going up in a complicated frame. The second one showed an old guy who was working on a building up in the sky.

Behind him was a city and a river. She knew one of the buildings. She had seen it in her parents' book of New York's skyscrapers. On an empty stomach, just looking at the picture made her feel dizzy. Uncle Ben came in from the kitchen.

"So what building do you think that guy is working on?" he asked.

"I don't know. But I've seen that other one with the pointy top before," she said, pointing to the tower in the background.

"That's the Chrysler Building and you'll go and see the one he's sitting on tomorrow. It doesn't look like that any more, but I'll give you a tip: it's the tallest building in New York."

"The Empire State Building?"

"You got it!"

"I can't believe he's just sitting out there with no safety belt. I mean if he fell ..."

"I know what you mean, that kind of work certainly isn't for everybody. See the river, that's where we ..."

Just then Rick and Basti entered the room.

"Ready to go, Zoe?" Rick asked. Zoe didn't know how to tell Rick that his father was just explaining something to her. That was just too much English for her on her first day. She looked up helplessly at her uncle.

"Viel Spaß!" he said, as if reading her mind.

"Debbie!" screamed Rick. "Get off the phone and come on!"

"Where are we going?" asked Debbie as they entered the elevator.

"Outside, where else?" said Rick sarcastically. Basti held back a smile but Zoe barely noticed. She was feeling hungry and was sorry that she hadn't accepted Aunt Marion's offer of something to eat.

They took a path to the Battery Park promenade: there were old-fashioned street lamps along the river and lots of old trees. Kids and adults on roller blades and skateboards raced by. They went up to look out over the dark blue water of the Hudson River. A styrofoam cup, a few soda cans, and a bright orange plastic bag were bouncing up and down on the river's short choppy waves.

"The water doesn't look very clean," said Basti.

"No, it really isn't. You wouldn't catch me swimming in it. My dad told me that a friend once took a trip with his canoe from Uptown Manhattan to Battery Park. Although he never fell in the water, he still got funny red spots on his legs and arms from the water that splashed on him."

"That's awful!" said Debbie.

"Well, that's what dad said."

"There's the Statue of Liberty," said Basti, pointing out across the river.

"Yup. There's the one and only original," said Rick with a proud smile. "Dad took us when I was about eight years old. That was back in 2000. Did you see the picture in our living room – the one that looks like a metal spiderweb?" Rick looked at Basti, but Zoe answered excitedly.

"I did, I saw it!" she said. "I was wondering what it was."

"Well, that's a picture of the spiral staircase inside the statue, which takes you all the way up to her crown. Up there, there are windows so that you can look out and see New York City," explained Rick.

Basti and Zoe stared out across the river. They squinted their eyes to block the strong sunshine which made it hard to see the statue's body clearly.

"Is that the boat you take?" asked Basti pointing to a big oval shaped boat with three levels.

"Yes, that's the one," answered Rick.

"I love riding on that ferry boat – the city looks so cool from the middle of the river," added Debbie.

Rick turned to Zoe and Basti. "After 9/11 you know, the day of the terror attacks, they closed the statue and you even needed a special pass just to go to the island. But this summer it opened again. We could go up there – if we get tickets."

"Are you sure it's open?" asked Debbie.

"Sure I'm sure. Dad said so."

"Why did they close it?" asked Basti.

"I guess they thought that, because it's a symbol of America, it might be a target for another attack," said Rick. He surprised even himself that he knew so much about the topic.

"How about the Empire State Building?" asked Zoe, remembering the photo in the Meyers' living room.

"I don't know for sure, but I think you can still go up. Dad will know."

"Well, he said that we would go tomorrow," said Zoe.

"Then there's no problem. Hey, maybe we should go back," suggested Rick lifting up Zoe's wrist to check the time.

They started walking back towards the Meyers' apartment building. "Isn't Ground Zero near here?" Zoe asked as if remembering something.

"Sure, it's just a little further than our house. I guess it would take us ten minutes to get there."

"You live that close? Wow!" said Basti.

"We probably still have enough time to go and check it out, if you like."

Zoe looked at Basti.

"I'm up for it," he said. Zoe was still feeling a bit dizzy, but no way was she going to stay behind.

"Me too," she added.

"OK, let's go. We just keep on walking down along the river."

"Where were you on that day?" asked Basti.

"What? What day?" asked Rick turning to Basti as if he had not quite heard his question. "Oh, you mean September 11, 2001." Basti nodded. Rick turned away from Basti and paused a moment as if trying to put things in order in his mind. Meanwhile, Basti was busy making a little calculation: 9/11 was eight years ago, so if Rick is 16 now, he was only seven or eight at the time.

"It's a long story. Are you ready for that?"

"Yeah, why not?" answered Basti.

"I was in school that morning. My school was called P.S. 89 and it's on Warren Street, just four blocks south of the World Trade Center Towers. We could see them out of our classroom window. They were always there. Our teacher, Mrs. Darnell, was talking about the dinosaur project that we were going to start the week after when I heard a loud bang. The assistant teacher, Miss Yang, looked out the window and let out a small scream. There was no way our teacher could stop all of us from getting up from our desks and running to the windows. I saw a big hole in one of the towers with fire shooting out. Then the second plane flew into the other tower. Some of the kids got really scared and started crying. The teachers told us all to sit down and said everything would be fine, and that it was just a little fire. Man, we sure weren't stupid enough to believe that! Mrs. Darnell started talking very quickly about dinosaur eggs and fossils, but nobody was listening. There was a lot of running around and shouting outside in the corridor. Another teacher came into our room and said we all had to go up to the gym on the third floor. Up in the gym the whole school watched a movie until our moms or dads came to pick us up. I remember Debbie didn't want to leave when mom came because she wanted to see the end of the movie! When my mom saw me, she started crying and squeezed me so hard, I could hardly breathe! We left the building and started walking towards the Battery Park promenade. The whole time mom wouldn't let go of my hand. She was just squeezing and squeezing. When we got to the promenade we waited in a long line to get on the next ferry. A lot of people were running by us. Some were bleeding, lots of people were crying and shouting. Police and ambulance sirens were going on and on.

Whenever I had the chance, I turned to look back at the towers. Black smoke was pouring out. It was a bright sunny day, but the air was so full of smoke that it looked like a storm was coming. It was hard to see and the air smelled really bad. I saw when the first tower collapsed. In seconds it was gone. Nobody could believe it. Then the second tower came down. It was about two hours after the planes had first hit." Rick paused a moment and looked down the promenade in the direction of the World Trade Center site.

"You can't imagine what that is like," he went on. "I mean, every day of my life I saw those two buildings a hundred times. They were just always there – outside my window, when I was going to school or ..." Rick stopped suddenly. A small tear rolled down his cheek. He wiped it away on his shirt sleeve. Basti looked down at the ground. He had been listening very carefully and waited until Rick went on with his story.

"Then we were on a ferry to Staten Island. That's the island across the river, over there." Rick pointed out onto the Hudson River to a piece of land way out on the horizon. I didn't go back into my room or my school for about six months. We stayed at my aunt's house in Staten Island and went to a school there. My mom and dad were only allowed to go back in the apartment for about four hours to pick up some stuff – things like clothes, passports. It was a crazy time. My mom was upset and nervous most of the time. I didn't always understand why. All the adults looked so sad. The TV was on a lot. I think what scared me most was the fire – a huge building on fire and people burning to death. I kept having bad dreams about it. And then seeing all the injured people, you know with blood on their faces and ..."

Just then Zoe and Debbie came running up.

"Hey guys, we were just at the Ground Zero Site – it's so cool. You have to see this: the rock they've dug up is amazing!" said Zoe showing them a picture of the underground site on her digital camera.

Chapter 2

Zoe woke up to the sound of the air-conditioner. Where was she? The air touching her body was strangely cold. She thought, this must be what it is like to be a vegetable in a fridge. She looked over to Debbie. Her face was hidden. In the dark, she could only see the mass of her wavy hair on the pillow. She looked at her watch: 5:00 am.

Hmm … nobody will be up yet, she thought. She turned back the covers, quietly got her camera out of her bag and hung it around her neck. She tip-toed out of the room, carefully closing the door behind her. She walked as softly as possible down the corridor, past the sound of Uncle Ben's snoring, past Rick's room and into the living room. She breathed a sigh of relief. Sunlight was already brightening up the room. Zoe went past the black sofa, the two armchairs and right out onto the balcony. Outside it was much warmer than the air-conditioned apartment. She looked out onto the Hudson River. It was touched with traces of gold and orange light. Far out on the river, the Statue of Liberty's arm reaching up into the morning sky was also touched by the golden-orange sunlight. She raised her camera and carefully framed a view of the statue. Below she heard the footsteps of a jogger running along the promenade. Who else was out this early in the morning? She saw a man with a lot of dirty, tangled hair on his head pushing a shopping cart. The cart was full with plastic bags and old clothes. Further down, two garbage men were emptying the garbage cans. A young woman on roller blades with a dog on a leash raced by and two old people sat together on one of the benches that faced the river. Zoe went back inside. She had taken about ten pictures and felt proud of herself. Professional photographers often wake up at strange times to get the right shot in the right light, she thought.

On her way back into Debbie's room, she passed by the photo of the Empire State Building under construction and looked at it through her own camera. She studied how the view of the city behind the unfinished building was less sharp than the man working in the foreground.

After a while she felt as if she were taking the photo of the city herself. She looked at her watch again: 6:05 am, New York time. She quietly walked down the corridor and slipped back into her cool bed in Debbie's room.

"OK, kids, here's today's plan: Empire State Building, Times Square at 42nd Street and a walk down Broadway with a stop for lunch and drinks. We were going to come with you, but we thought you four musketeers would have more fun without us. I'm going to print tickets for you from the Internet, but first let's take a look at the route." Uncle Ben spread out two maps on the kitchen table. Zoe read: New York City Subway Map and Map of Manhattan. Uncle Ben started with the subway map. "Here we are. This used to be our station but it's been closed since 9/11. So you'll need to walk down to the Rector Street station, here." He pointed to a black circle on a long red line that ran all along the long side of Manhattan island. "This is the 7th Avenue Local line," he went on, "you take the number 1 train up to 34th Street – Penn Station, then walk east on 34th Street, past 6th Avenue to 5th Avenue. And – *voilà*! The Empire State Building. It's the tallest building in New York, so you really can't miss it." Uncle Ben then opened the street map.

"After your trip up to the top, and back down, I suggest you walk up Broadway to 42nd Street. Take a look at Times Square and if you are all up for it, start walking back downtown on Broadway. You could stop anywhere and get on a subway or you can walk all the way back." Uncle Ben showed the route by drawing his finger along the street named Broadway – the only diagonal street to cross the regular grid of streets. To Basti, New York City looked like a place where it was almost impossible to get lost. There were no curving streets and almost all the streets were numbered. And just in case you started feeling lost, you could look up and see one of the tallest buildings in the world.

☆

Zoe walked down the corridor and heard laughter coming from Rick's room. She stood in front for a few moments and then knocked on the door.

"Yeah?" said Rick's voice.

"It's me, Zoe, can I come in?"

"Sure, Zoe, come on in," answered Rick swinging open the door. A strange smell tickled Zoe's nose – it was something like the smell of old pajamas. She looked around. What a mess compared to Debbie's room, she thought. His table was made by an old piece of wood laid over two file cabinets. The table had a clip-on lamp. There were some papers and two school textbooks on his desk: American History, and Algebra and a school book: *Of Mice and Men*.

His desk was pulled away from the wall. He had a bookshelf behind the desk and leaning on the shelf was a keyboard. The bookshelf didn't have that many books: it had a complete collection of *Lord of the Rings*, books on skateboarding technique and two *Harry Potter* novels. There were also some old DVDs – *Star Wars*, *Bat Man*, and all the

Lord of the Rings films – an old Lego ship collecting dust, a basketball and a stack of frisbees. On top of the shelf were two basketball trophies and a black bag. There were also a lot of cables under the table. Unlike Debbie's room, there were no posters on the wall. There was just one long photograph above his bed of a subway train painted with graffiti. Zoe didn't exactly know where to sit. Rick was sitting in his rotating desk chair, turning from side to side and Basti was sitting cross-legged on the bed. The bed was covered with stickers. Each one was a little bit different. They looked as if they had been drawn by hand. She sat down next to her brother and picked up one sticker next to her leg. "What are these?" she asked.

"Rick made them," said Basti. "They are street stickers."

"Yeah, my friends and I make them and stick them all over the city – you know on garbage cans, lamp posts, and sometimes on mailboxes, subway walls and benches. We each have a character and a special signature. My name is *The Borg*. Look, here is a Borg," said Rick.

"Cool," said Zoe "Did you make all of these?" she asked.

"No, my friends made some."

"You just go up to a lamp post or wall and stick it on? Don't you get into trouble if somebody sees you doing that?" asked Zoe.

"Well, first of all, we don't do it on a busy street or if it looks like people will see us. But, still, a few months ago an old guy, maybe he was about 70 years old or something, caught me putting one on a lamp post. He got so angry! He kept on shouting at me: 'What do you think you're doing? This is public property!' He also told me he was going to call the police. Two of my friends were with me. We just ran away as fast as we could."

"Some people think it's uncool, but I think it gives life to lamp posts and garbage cans," said Rick, picking up one of his stickers and looking at it lovingly.

"Are you guys ready yet?" asked Marion, popping her head into Rick's room. "Dad is just printing out the tickets. Rick, come over here a moment. Here is some money for lunch, darling," she said handing Rick a 20 and a 10 dollar bill. "I'm also going to give you an extra $10, just in case. By the way, where is Debbie?"

"I think she's in the bathroom," answered Zoe from Rick's room.

"Typical," said Rick. "She spends hours in there." Aunt Marion gave him a look which seemed to say, "Behave yourself!" Just then Uncle Ben came tunneling down the corridor saying in his usual loud voice, "I can't believe the price of these tickets: $18 for an elevator ride!"

Aunt Marion hurried up to her husband trying to quiet him and then whispered in his ear, "Hey Ben, please don't talk about the price in front of the kids. I don't want them to feel guilty or nervous about the cost. Let them enjoy themselves! They don't get a chance to be with one another very often."

But Zoe and Basti had heard Uncle Ben. Zoe quickly calculated the cost of all four of them: $72. Wow, that's a lot of money! She made a note in her mind to bring them back some great photos.

☆

"There it is," said Debbie. "Dum-ta-ta-tum! The one and only Empire State Building!"

"Let me just run across the street to take a picture. I'll be right back," said Zoe, excitedly.

Zoe ran across the street. At least ten other tourists had the same idea. *"Is' ja blöd,"* said Zoe to herself. Even from across the street, her back against a building, she wasn't able to fit the whole building into one shot. It was just too tall. She dropped her camera and looked at the other tourists – maybe they knew a trick that she hadn't yet learned. She tried to form the question in her mind: 'Can you see the whole building on your camera?' or was it 'Can you see the total building with your camera?' … or 'in your camera' … The more she thought about it the shyer she felt and when she heard her name being called, she was happy to forget about the whole thing and to run back across the street to the others.

☆

They entered the lobby. A picture of the tower in gold glowed from the back wall and an American flag was hanging on each side.

"It's a good thing we've already got our tickets – look at that line!" said Debbie. It was true. The line for tickets to the observation deck was long and slow moving. But the line for the elevators was just as long.

"I can't believe this," said Rick. "It looks like every tourist in Manhattan decided to visit the Empire State Building today." A Japanese tour group was in front of them, and a kid's birthday party group behind.

"I just want to go and get some chewing gum for the elevator ride. I'll be right back," said Debbie and disappeared. Rick got on the end of the line while Zoe and Basti picked up a brochure in German about the building. The line snaked around and around. People in line were speaking German, Spanish, Japanese, French, a Scandinavian language and of course English.

Debbie came back smiling. Zoe, Basti and Rick were only about ten feet closer to the elevators. She gave a piece of gum to her cousins and brother. The women in the Japanese group were fanning themselves with the *General Information* brochures, while the parents of the birthday boy organized a game of 'telephone' in order to keep the ten eight-year-olds in line. Finally they were in the elevator. The trip up was space-age. They zoomed up to the 80th floor. The elevator was moving so fast it felt like it was shaking. Zoe was glad that Debbie had given her that piece of gum. Her ears were popping in the way they did when a plane takes off or lands. She looked over at Basti. He was chewing his gum with concentration. They arrived at the 80th floor and then got on another elevator which took them to the 86th floor observation deck. There were a lot of people up there and it took a bit of pushing to get to a free spot. But, when they did … Wow! There was so much city to see. Zoe was all over the place. It was hard to decide whether to take pictures or just to look at the view with her own eyes. Basti was interested in the drawings of important buildings that one could see from specific spots along the balcony. Sky, river, streets stretching out into the horizon and buildings, buildings, buildings.

"I can see the curve of the Earth from up here!" shouted Rick.

"No way! You probably just need glasses," said Debbie.

"No really – come on – can't you see that slight curve when you look out as far as you can? Just try it …"

"Well, kind of … I … it's hard to tell," said Debbie not wanting to admit that Rick was right.

"Basti! There you are!" she said as she pressed herself next to him.

"What?" he said, his finger on the diagram where he was trying to find the next building.

"See that big green area over there?" said Basti.

"That's Central Park," said Rick. "It's a really great place for frisbee, skateboarding and …"

"You can also go to outdoor rock concerts," said Debbie.

"That's not what I was going to say, actually," her brother snapped back quickly.

"OK, what were you going to say?" asked Debbie.

"I don't remember now. I hate it when other people finish my sentences! So don't do it!"

"Hey, cool down, Rick, I didn't mean it in a bad way," said Debbie, clearly not wanting to start an argument in front of her cousins and certainly not on top of the Empire State Building.

"Do you think we can see your house from up here?" asked Basti.

"I don't know, but, we'll have to go over there to check," said Rick and pointed around the corner of the look-out platform. They stayed up on the platform for another half an hour trying to find the Meyers' apartment building and arguing about whether or not they could actually see Ground Zero. When Debbie finally suggested that she thought it was time to go back down to street level, no one argued.

☆

Rick and Basti were walking down Broadway, ahead of Debbie and Zoe. They were walking quickly, like everybody else. It was the New York walk – walking as if you have a very important appointment in a few minutes' time. They passed shop after shop and restaurant after restaurant. Sneakers, clothes, electronic equipment, pizza, bagels, fast food, burgers and fries. Rick suddenly pointed to a lamp post on the corner of 33rd Street and Broadway.

"Look at that sticker!" said Rick pointing to a picture of something that looked like a kid with a baseball cap. "That's one of my friend Moog's stickers. He puts them up all over the city. Last night I got a call from Moog. Tomorrow they want to go down to this tunnel that nobody uses any more. I've never been, but I've heard that there are great paintings and graffiti on the walls. Moog and I have been talking about doing something of our own. I've already got the spray paint. Do you want to go?" asked Rick.

"Of course! That sounds great!" said Basti.

"But what do we do about your sister? I mean, my mom and dad can't know that we're going down there. We have to keep it a secret, OK. Maybe she and Debbie can do something together. I don't know, what do you think?" Basti didn't answer right away. He had to think. Of course Zoe could keep a secret. He was also thinking about what his dad had said … that Aunt Marion and Uncle Ben should know where we are at all times. And why didn't Rick want his parents to know that he was going into this tunnel? Was it dangerous or illegal? But Rick would have his cellphone, argued Basti with himself.

"Does your cellphone work down in the tunnel?" asked Basti – and a second later wished he had asked a different question.

"Well, I've never tried, but I guess so. Why?" he asked, smiling.

"I mean … uh … if anything went wrong … could we make a call? I mean, is it dangerous down there?"

"Well, I would say it's not the safest place in the world. There are quite a few rats, but my friends have gone down there many times and nothing has ever happened to them." Both Rick and Basti turned around to see where Zoe and Debbie were. They had stopped in front of a store and Zoe was pointing at something in the window display.

"I had to promise dad that I would watch out for Zoe. If I go, I guess she has to go too," said Basti quietly.

"That's hard to understand. You have to watch out for her the whole time you're here? That's a pretty bad deal if you ask me!"

Basti was silent.

"OK – if that is how it has to be, I'd say we go and get some lunch and talk it over with the girls – see what they want to do. And anyway, I'm starved!" They both shouted their sisters' names above the noise of the traffic. Zoe and Debbie came running up.

"What's wrong?" asked Debbie.

"Nothing we're just starving," said Rick.

"So are we! Let's find a place to eat. How about pizza?" said Debbie.

"Pizza! Yes, I love pizza and I want to try New York Pizza." Zoe was pointing to a restaurant across the street with a big sign which read "New York Pizza".

☆

"What are you doing tomorrow, Deb?" asked Rick, following a string of melted cheese that got ever longer the more he pulled the slice of pizza away from his mouth.

Debbie narrowed her eyes – she found Rick's question very suspicious.

"What do you mean? I thought we were all doing something together."

"Well, yeah, but I just wanted to know if you have any ideas what that something may be," explained Rick.

"I think we should ask Basti and Zoe what they would like to do. I mean, mom wrote down a list of interesting places to visit and we could just pick one of those," answered Debbie with a very practical tone.

"I have an idea," said Rick taking a sharp, quick look at each of the others.

"Why didn't you just say so in the beginning, then?" said Debbie exasperated.

"Shh ... just listen. Moog, Raul and I want to explore a place called the Freedom Tunnel. And we want to do that tomorrow. We're meeting at the 125th Street Station near Riverside Park and the tunnel entrance. Basti wants to come. There's some of the greatest graffiti in the world down there. I'm taking my spray paints. We want to do our own. We can all go, but – and this is a big but – not one of you must whisper a word about this to mom or dad." Rick looked at the others. No one said a word.

"What do you say?" he asked.

"What kind of tunnel is it? I mean, is it dangerous? Do cars drive through?" asked Basti, his face turning red.

Zoe's heart was beating fast. Was this one of the dangerous things dad had warned them about?

"No. No cars … It was a tunnel for trains. I think it starts at Penn Station. Trains used to run through, but now it's closed. As far as I know, no trains run down there any more. A while ago, I guess in the 1980s, a lot of homeless people lived down there. Some even built houses inside the tunnel. Also lots of artists went down there to paint their graffiti on the walls. And I mean some of the best graffiti artists in the world! We want to paint our stuff there, too. I've never been down there, but I've been to other old stations and I think it's just something you've got to experience while you're here." And turning to Zoe, Rick went on, "You've got a camera, right? You could take the coolest pictures down there. Everybody has a picture of the Empire State Building, but this would be something really special."

Zoe's heart started beating even faster. She was thinking of the photo of the subway car in Rick's room and the photograph of the inside of the Statue of Liberty: both were really great shots. "I think we should go," she said quietly.

"Me too," said Basti.

Debbie looked like she was still thinking it over. She thought Moog was pretty strange.

"I don't know if I want to come … do homeless people still live there?"

"No, not like before. They were kicked out … I can even show you some pictures of it on Wikipedia," said Rick. He was trying to make the tunnel as attractive as possible.

"Well …"

"Come on, Deb! Don't be a party pooper!" said Rick throwing up his arms.

"All right, all right, I'll come. But there'd better not be any rats down there!" she said.

"No, of course not!" Rick said looking directly at Basti.

"One last thing. We'll take a look at the maps tomorrow morning after mom and dad leave for work. And don't forget – if they ask you where we're going tomorrow, just say we're going to Central Park, maybe the zoo or the Metropolitan Museum of Art. We can even stop there on the way back so you guys don't have to lie. Ok?"

Chapter 3

"Moog and Raul are going to meet us here at the 125th Street Station Uptown platform at 10:30," said Rick landing his finger firmly down in a northern part of the Manhattan map.

"125th is the beginning of Harlem. See, it's also called Martin Luther King Jr. Boulevard," added Debbie.

"Thanks for the geography lesson, Deb, now let me go on. We get out at the back of the train, meet Moog and Raul, and walk west along Tiemann Place. At the end of the street, we cross a little park here, cross another street that's called Riverside Drive and now here comes the hard part: we'll have to climb over a fence here."

"A fence?" asked Zoe.

"Yeah, it's one of those metal park fences. It's not too high, and it's pretty easy to climb over, but I think it's better if we all wear trousers and sneakers, OK? Then it might be a little rough going because the park slopes down here before we get to the tunnel entrance. See the train tracks here? The tunnel begins right after that. Above the tunnel is a park, but nobody up there really knows what's going on down below. It's a cool feeling to know that. I've read that you can hear kids playing right above your head. Anyway, when we're at the tunnel entrance, we wait for one train to go by –"

"Trains? I thought you said that the tunnel is closed and no more trains go through," said Basti, worried again that they might be doing something that was really too dangerous.

"Well, yeah, I was wrong. But there is only one train that goes by every 40 minutes. We've got to be careful, but it's really not a problem. That's why I think we should wait for one train to pass by before we go into the tunnel. That way we'll have some time to explore before the next one comes. We wait outside, and as it's passing, we all check our watches. Does each of you have a watch?" Basti, Deb and Zoe all held up their hands.

"And are they all on New York time?" Rick looked at Basti and Zoe.

"Of course!" said Zoe.

"Oops – mine is not … it says quarter to three."

"OK, change that to 8:45."

"The important thing is that we're all far from the tracks when the next train comes through. That's the only really dangerous part. These trains go fast. We have to be prepared to move away from the tracks even before we hear one coming. We also don't want the train driver to see us. Is this all clear to you?" said Rick looking up from the map. Debbie, Zoe and Basti nodded.

"Any other questions?"

"Do trains go by every 40 minutes in both directions? I mean at the same time?" asked Basti.

"That's a good question … But I don't really know the answer," said Rick. "Anything else?" There was a moment of silence.

"Good. OK, what to take? I think we should all take a bottle of water and a flashlight." Rick went to the hallway closet and brought back two large flashlights. "Here, Basti and Zoe, why don't you take these. They're a bit big, but they're strong. Debbie, you have one in your room, right?"

"Yeah, I guess so …" said Debbie, sounding a bit far away as though she was thinking of something else.

"Great. I'll take my spray paints and some stickers. You guys are welcome to try them out if you like. OK. I think that's it. Debbie and I will clean up here, you guys can go and get ready."

"I'm not going with you," said Debbie after Zoe and Basti had left the room.

"What? You don't want to come with us?"

"Yes, that's what I said – I'm staying here," said Debbie in a soft voice.

"What are you talking about?"

"I've got other things to do and I just don't want to go. Your friends give me a hard time and it's just not my kind of thing. I don't want to see all that garbage and graffiti. I'm not like you. I'm not an 'urban guerrilla'."

"What did you just call me? An urban guerrilla? What is that supposed to mean? We just like exploring places that other people don't know about … that's all," said Rick. "I'm not hurting anybody."

"We don't have to argue about it. I just don't want to go. I can meet you guys later on."

"What are you going to tell mom?"

"Nothing. I'll meet you in Central Park and we can come home together. I can even bring a picnic. It's really not a big deal. How about 1 pm?"

"OK, if that's the way you want it. But why don't *you* go tell Basti and Zoe? And – if you say a word of this to mom, you are dead meat!"

"Rick, you don't have to threaten me, you know!" shouted Debbie, storming out of the kitchen. Basti was in Rick's room, and Zoe was in the bathroom, but they all heard the door slam shut.

☆

"Next stop: 125th Street – Martin Luther King Boulevard," said the voice over the speakers. It had been a long slow ride on the Uptown local train and they were all standing in front of the doors, ready to get off when the train pulled into the station.

"Moog, Raul! Hey, man!" yelled Rick to the two boys who walked towards them. Rick came up to a chubby but tall boy and they gave each other a soul shake: they touched forearms then slid down to their hands, ending in a hook action with three of their fingers. Rick's friend was wearing a big white T-shirt and long, baggy cargo shorts. He was smiling as if he was ready to tell a joke. The other boy was wearing a black woolen hat and was even taller and skinnier than Basti. He walked up to Rick and performed the same greeting, adding a shoulder bump to the mix.

"These are my cousins, Basti and Zoe," said Rick.

"Hi, I'm Moog and this is Raul," he said and put out his hand. "You guys live in Germany, right?"

"Yes, we live in Darmstadt – it's close to Frankfurt. You know Frankfurt?" asked Basti.

"I know frankfurters – you know the kind you can eat – hot dogs," said Moog and laughed.

"Well, we are Frankfurters ... but not that kind. We call hot dogs *Wiener Würstchen* – have you ever heard of them?" asked Basti.

"Yeah, yeah – we sometimes call hot dogs wieners, but I've never heard that other word, what was it ... worst-chain?"

"Yes, something like that," said Basti laughing.

"OK, we can continue with the language lesson later. I think we should head out now while the sun is still high," said Raul and started to walk towards the stairs.

They followed the exit signs for Tiemann Place and walked along the street just like Rick had said. They reached the cross street and entered the first small park. They crossed a larger double-lane street called Riverside Drive and then jogged across the second park. They could already see the Hudson River from this point which was just beyond a highway.

"OK guys, now comes the hard part. We've got to climb over this fence and then slide down the slope on the other side. There might be rocks and broken glass – so watch where you step. Moog, why don't you go first, then Zoe, Raul and Basti and I will go last," said Rick in a serious tone.

"Ay-ay Captain," said Moog teasingly. Moog went over first and then stood on the other side, waiting. Zoe tucked her camera into her shirt before she grabbed the fence. She did quite well climbing up, but was confused when she got to the top of the fence.

"Just lift one leg over!" shouted Rick.

"I'll catch you on this side …" said Moog, "or you can jump, it's not that far."

Zoe chose jumping – better than landing in Moog's arms, she thought. She landed with a bit too much force and ended up with dirt on her knees and hands.

Basti, Raul and Rick went over quite easily, and did the soul shakes with Moog after landing. They walked across a small green area to the tracks below. There was garbage everywhere: bottles, cans, cigarette butts and plastic bags.

"That's the tunnel entrance," said Moog pointing to a dark, square opening with grass and even small trees growing on top. They walked along a gravel path next to the tracks until they reached the tunnel opening.

"I think we should wait here for a train to go by," said Rick.

"Really, man?" said Raul, shaking his head.

"Yeah, come on, Rick. If one just passed by, we might have to wait here another half an hour," added Moog kicking a few bits of gravel towards the metal tracks.

"Well, I don't think one just went by. We would have heard it. We weren't that far away. And besides [illegible] is Basti and Zoe's first time down here and their second [illegible] w York! If anything happens, man, it will be my faul[illegible] t to make it as safe as possible," said Rick, kicking a few more pebbles at the tracks.

"Rick – you, Zoe and I could also wait here. Moog and Raul should go ahead if they want," suggested Basti.

"I don't ..." – whatever Rick was going to say, the thundering sound of an approaching train was cutting him off. The five kids jumped back into the green area just as the train raced by, kicking gravel and dust into the air. It blew its horn as if to say: I know you kids are there. As soon as the train passed, Moog started running into the tunnel screaming like a madman.

"Stop! Wait!" shouted Rick, but Moog didn't turn back. "We should all check our watches. It's 11:05 now. That means the next train will be at 11:45. OK?"

"OK OK ... now, let's get going!" said Raul impatiently, shifting his backpack on his back and taking a few wide strides into the tunnel. "Wow!" he screamed, "look at that light!" The tunnel was about 6 meters high and 18 meters wide. Although it was bright and sunny outside, the tunnel was very dark. About every 20 meters, sunlight from openings above cut into the tunnel's thick darkness. You could almost touch the light with your fingers.

"Oooh eeee!" That was Moog and the tunnel echoed back and made funny changes to his voice.

Raul tried out his voice with a loud "Hellooooo, hellooo ...," then Zoe echoed him, "Haaaaallo, haaaallo ..." Then all three were calling out. They passed under an opening in the roof of the tunnel.

"Hold on!" Basti yelled out. "Can't they hear us up above if we're making so much noise?"

"Yeah, I think you're right. We shouldn't be screaming like this," said Rick. Everybody fell silent.

Crunch, crunch, crunch was the sound of the stones under their feet as they went deeper into the tunnel. Gravel and dirt mixed with all kinds of garbage that covered the ground next to the tracks. There were empty cans of spray paint, old clothes, shoes, blankets, and plastic dolls with dirty faces. The air became cooler and had a strange smell of rusty metal, machine oil, old garbage and earth. The colors that had filled their eyes that morning were gone: the green of the trees, the blue sky, and the bright sunlight. Now there were the grays, browns and blacks of this underworld. Color appeared only in the explosion of graffiti on the tunnel walls. Zoe had never seen such amazing graffiti. As they walked on, she would stop just long enough to take photos without falling too far behing from the rest of the group. Small white signs on the walls marked the street numbers above: 119th St., 118th ...

When Raul and Moog found an empty section of wall, they set down their bags, took out their paints and started shaking the cans. Rick, Basti and Zoe stopped to watch. Soon the two boys were doing a kind of hip hop dance in front of the wall while spraying on their names. Moog wasn't Moog's real name. He shared it with the rabbit robot character that

Zoe had seen on some of Rick's stickers. As the rabbit's ears and face began to appear on the tunnel wall, Rick, Zoe and Basti walked on into the darkness of the tunnel. To the left and to the right colorful graffiti burst out from the walls.

"Man, this is great stuff!" said Rick. "There should also be real paintings down here. Here! Look at this!" Rick jumped in front of a long wall painting that was over three meters high and about 30 meters long. It was awesome. The wall painting was divided up into different sections, just like a comic strip. Two of these sections showed faces in black and white – faces which seemed to come out of the darkness of the tunnel. Other sections were painted with the red and white stripes of the American flag. The last section had the words: 'There's no way like the American way' in a beautiful white script.

You just had to stop for a moment and imagine an artist painting this huge work in this dark place. He would have to bring down paints, brushes, a ladder even. It must be difficult to paint on the rough surface of the tunnel wall – and to paint so well.

"This is a painting by a guy who called himself 'Freedom'," explained Rick. "The tunnel is named after him. I've read about him on the Internet. His real name is Chris Pape and he even lived down here for a while. There are a lot more of his paintings further down in the tunnel," said Rick. He realized that he sounded like a museum guide who explains the artwork to a small group of tourists. So he quickly said, "Now I need to find a good place to do my own work." The best places directly under the light from above were all taken.

"How about here?" suggested Basti and stopped. He pointed to an area where somebody had started a graffiti but not finished it. The wall was white in some places, but there was still a large area that was untouched.

"That's great, Basti," said Rick excitedly. He dropped his bag and took out all of his spray cans.

"Can you start shaking some of these? You can also use them if you want. You could even just write 'Basti the Frankfurter, 2009'!"

"I'll just start with the shaking," said Basti.

"I'm going to walk on and take some more pictures," said Zoe.

"Do you want me to come with you?" asked Basti vigorously shaking one of the cans.

"No, that's all right. I'll be back very soon, don't worry." Zoe took a sip of water from her bottle and headed out.

There was something very special about the light coming down from above. It was like a Star Wars laser-sword cutting through the tunnel's darkness. You could almost hold it in your hand. Zoe had only seen light like this a few times in her life. Maybe it was like that because the air in the tunnel was so still – there was absolutely no wind. Or maybe it was the dust hanging in the air, dust that each one of them kicked into the air with every step they took. The rhythm of light and darkness went on as far into the tunnel as she could see. At each spot where light entered, the wall below was washed in light. It was just like an art gallery or a museum, where strong spot lights light up the paintings on the walls. And there were paintings here, too – real paintings. Some were portraits: ghost-like faces in black and white. To Zoe, the faces looked hungry and poor as if they had a hard life. The white in their faces, Zoe thought, glows in the light. But probably for only a few hours every day. Then there are the long hours of darkness and stillness. Zoe shivered. There were also paintings that were copies of famous paintings she had seen in art books. Copies of Leonardo da Vinci, or was it Michelangelo? One had the face of an angel. Another was just the body of a woman and a man like those old Greek statues with no arms and no heads. She reached 107th Street – she knew because the sign on the wall told her. Below the little sign was the strangest painting she had seen yet. It was a picture of a figure in a black sweat jacket with a spray paint can for a head.

"Wow, komisch ..." she heard herself say out loud. And then it clicked – something she had not understood as she walked through this strange underground gallery. Were all of these awesome paintings done with spray paint? – simple cans of spray paint that other people use to paint old bikes? How did they do it? It was really amazing. She suddenly wanted to understand the technique. Even the graffiti began to look magical. Earlier she hadn't paid much attention to

the way Moog, Raul and Rick had drawn on the walls. Although some of the graffiti was great, it didn't really grab her like these paintings did. But – oh my God! What time is it? Zoe checked her watch. 11:35! She had been wandering alone for over 20 minutes so there must be another train soon. The others were blocks away. What did Rick say? Get as far away from the tracks as possible. Get out of sight of the train driver. Find a niche in the wall. Press yourself against the wall before the train comes. That means NOW! Zoe was scared – her hands were shaking. "I've got about eight minutes." She ran over the tracks to the wall. She tried to get around a pile of garbage, but by mistake she stepped on a soft and very dirty teddy bear that lay in her path. She saw an opening or door on the other side. Zoe ran over. There was a door. There were even a few steps leading up to it. Painted on the wall next to the door were the words 'Home Sweet Home'. No train can come up here, she thought and hopped up the steps. She pushed open the door and stepped in. It was totally dark inside the room. My flashlight! she thought happily and reached inside her backpack. Flick went the switch. She heard a sound. Movement. A little snort. With the light illuminating the little room, Zoe met eye to eye with an old man. He was sitting at a large metal desk and looked at her with a surprised look.

"*Entschuldigung! Ich* … I … I'm sorry …"

"German! You're German?!" said the man in a gruff voice. "Who are you?"

"My name is Zoe. I was just …"

"And you're German, right?"

☆

Basti looked at his watch. It was 11:35. They had been in the tunnel for about half an hour. The next train would be coming in less than ten minutes. Moog and Raul were putting the finishing touches on their graffiti. Rick had shown Basti how to use the spray paint and he had tried to sign his name on the wall as well. But where was Zoe? The last time he had seen her, she was standing in front of one of the longer paintings. She was trying to figure out how to get a good picture of the whole thing. That was at least ten minutes ago. He ran back to that spot. She wasn't there. He ran to Moog and Raul, who were starting to pack up their things. No sign of her.

"Have you seen Zoe?" he asked.

"No, I thought she was with you guys," Raul said. Basti ran back to Rick.

"Rick, I can't find Zoe. She must have wandered off and a train will be coming soon," said Basti nervously. "I've got to find her, now." He turned and started running deeper into the tunnel shouting her name.

Rick dropped the can he had in his hand. So far he had written 'BOR'. He quickly collected his paints, threw them into the bag and started running to catch up with Basti.

Basti turned around. There was Rick, gasping for air and holding out his hand and shouting, "Basti! BASTI! Wait!"

"Come on, Basti, let's stay together, and, don't worry, we would see her if she was on the tracks," said Rick trying to calm Basti down.

"Let's cross the tracks now, before the train comes. Do you see those doors on the other side? They must be storage rooms. Maybe she's gone into one of them."

Basti was starting to imagine the worst. Zoe kidnapped by a homeless person ... She's got that expensive camera hanging around her neck, how stupid could I have been to let her come down with that! I should have kept my eye on her, she's just fourteen … and now, mom and dad are going to kill me if anything happens to her …, thought Basti. Drops of sweat were starting to form on his forehead.

Up ahead they saw an old door held open by a piece of wood.

"Here, let's try this one," said Rick, kicking the wood aside and throwing the creaking door open.

There was nothing in the small room except an old sleeping bag, a broken cup and plate and a huge stack of old newspapers. No sign of Zoe. They ran down to the next, still shouting "Zoe, Zoe!" The next door was 50 meters down. There were a few crumbling steps leading to the door. This door had a handle. Just as they turned the handle, a train came thundering through the tunnel. Basti felt as if his heart would burst out of his chest.

☆

"There goes another one of those Amtrak trains. They're often late, you know," said an old man sitting at a metal desk. "The more expensive the ticket, the greater chance you can expect to arrive at least 20 minutes late." He looked up at the two boys. "Well, well, well, what do we have here? Two young men appearing out of nowhere. Running away from trains? You see, my young dear, I told you they would find you!"

"Zoe! You're here! We didn't know where you were … What a relief!" tears were coming to Basti's eyes.

"Hey, Basti, Rick – I want you to meet Mr. Kaminski," said Zoe smiling. "Mr. Kaminski, this is my brother Sebastian and my cousin Rick."

"Nice to meet you," said Basti, looking very confused but tending his hand towards the old man.

"Pleasure is mine, Sebastian. And you are Nick?"

"No – Rick."

"Oh Rick, you must excuse an old man's poor hearing. I don't always get it right the first time these days. But I did hear you call this little girl's name, of course. 'Zoe! Zoe!' We had a good laugh – poor young fellas, you thought you'd lost her, didn't you? It can be a dangerous place, of course. We all have to watch out for those trains. I've got something here, you see, that you might find interesting," continued Mr. Kaminski and pulled out a folded piece of paper from his shirt pocket. A hand-drawn table written in blue ink covered the sheet.

"It's a timetable I made myself. It lists the times of all the trains that pass by here – morning, day and night and on weekends, too. But as I was telling your little sister here, you can't always count on an Amtrak train being on time. Those new drivers have lost the touch. What do they care? For them, it's just a well paid job." Mr. Kaminski handed the timetable to Rick. The paper was soft from being folded and unfolded so many times. Zoe tells me you came all the way from Germany to visit us down in these deep catacombs. So, what do you fine boys think of our underground world? Anyone who has ever lived here and also most of the great artists who work here know me. They all call me the Professor! Hah! But I've never seen your faces before. Is this your first visit?" Mr. Kaminski spoke with a slight accent. Rick guessed it was a Polish or Russian accent, but he wasn't sure. Mr. Kaminski continued, "The young lady here tells me that you are from Germany, near Frankfurt. But tell me, young man, who brought you here? This old tunnel isn't usually part of the Big Apple tours!" Mr. Kaminski looked straight at Basti. Basti opened his mouth but nothing came out. It was strange, but he felt as if the old man had spoken to him in German. Suddenly Basti only had German in his mind although he had been speaking English every moment of the day since he had arrived. When he finally answered Mr. Kaminski's question, he was speaking neither English nor German, "*Ich* ... I mean, I come, came with my cousin. He is *von* here. He made graffiti ... sometimes ...."

Luckily, Rick came to the rescue and answered in a more confident voice. "They came down with me, Mr. Kaminski. I'm a graffiti artist and my friends have been here a few times before."

Mr. Kaminski listened carefully, scratched his head and began again.

"Boys, you have every right to be down here, just as much as I do, but I am a little worried. This little lady has a camera, does she not?" he asked, pointing to Zoe.

"Yes, sir," answered Rick.

"And, she is a bit younger than you two boys, is she not?"

"Yes, sir," answered both Rick and Basti, now that Basti was getting a better idea of how to talk to the old man.

"But you young gentlemen think it perfectly all right to let your younger sister walk around here alone with her camera and fresh off the plane from Germany, don't you?"

"Well ... she just disappeared."

"Please, boys, answer the question."

"Yes, sir, I-I mean, no, sir."

"My dear gentlemen, I might be a bit old-fashioned, but in my days we would never let our younger sisters out of our sight, especially not in a dark and dangerous place like this. I'm sure Zoe is very brave and that she doesn't want two boys always looking over her shoulder. But please, boys, this is New York. And we all want this young lady to grow up to be a famous photographer one day. Is that clear?"

"Yes, sir."

"Good. Now, please bring Zoe back to the rest of your group – such strange names they had – Moo like a cow, was it? And what was the other called? Raw? Rule? Raw what? Raw rule? … no, that doesn't sound right." Zoe went over to the old man to shake his hand.

"One more thing, boys, next time you are in the tunnel come and visit old Mr. Kaminski. I always like to hear what the young people think of the world outside. If you don't find me in my office with all my maps, just ask anybody if they've seen the Professor! Hah! They'll know who you mean. And take care of that sister of yours!"

As they left Mr. Kaminski's office, Basti was wondering if the old man climbed over the fence just as they had done, or if he had a special entrance. Or did Mr. Kaminski live in the tunnel? What did he actually do in his 'office'? It was all so strange. Rick had other things on his mind. He hadn't had enough time to finish his graffiti, but now it was already past 12 o'clock, and he had told Debbie that they would meet her at 1. They had to leave the tunnel straight away. As they passed the spot on the wall where he had been working, Rick told himself that he had to come back and finish.

Moog and Raul were taking a break from their graffiti action painting when Rick, Basti and Zoe arrived.

"So, you found her," said Moog, "It's good to know that she wasn't run over by a train," he added, smiling and laughing at Zoe's expense. She decided she really didn't like Moog. He was mean, although his jokes were sometimes pretty funny.

"Hey man, it looks awesome," said Rick. He was carefully looking at their graffiti that still had that strong smell of spray paint. "But we've got to leave now. I told my sister Debbie we would meet her in Central Park at 1. How long are you guys going to stay?"

"We're staying until we're finished. We're not tourists," said Raul picking up a can of black paint.

"... I wish I could stay, but that's the way it goes. I'll be back."

They did their soul shake again and Zoe, Rick and Basti headed towards the bright light at the tunnel's opening.

Chapter 4

Zoe realized how tired she was as they climbed up the steps to 72nd Street from the subway station below. As they walked down 72nd Street, Zoe saw a lot of things she would have liked to photograph: people, restaurants, bagel shops ... But she was just too tired and hungry. It had been an exciting, strange and even scary morning. Rick, who had been very quiet the whole subway ride, suddenly said, "Wow, am I hungry."

Zoe looked up and saw a strip of green at the end of the street.

"And on your right," said Rick in a tourist guide voice, "is the most famous apartment building in New York, The Dakota, where former Beatle John Lennon was shot dead as he was walking towards that gate." He was pointing to a high black gate in the old building. They crossed a big street called Central Park West and entered the park.

Debbie was sitting on a bench not far from a green sign which read 'Strawberry Fields'. Next to her was a big backpack. She was reading a book and didn't see her cousins and brother until they were standing right above her and Rick said, "Boo!"

Debbie, totally surprised, let out a little scream.

"Hey, you almost gave me a heart attack!" She pulled out her earphones.

"What are you listening to?" asked Rick smiling, "Give Peace a Chance?"

"Ha ha. Very funny, Rick!" Basti and Zoe walked towards Debbie.

Debbie closed her book and switched off her mp3 player. "Anyway, ... how was it?"

"What? You mean the tunnel?" asked Rick.

"Yes, of course – what else?"

"I took a lot of photos ... the graffiti and the paintings down there are really great, but it gets pretty scary when the trains come."

"That's right," added Rick, "especially when you walk off by yourself."

"Well, you guys were so busy with your graffiti. And I wanted to see more of the tunnel," said Zoe in her defense.

"What? I don't understand," said Debbie.

"Zoe got lost ..." said Basti.

"No, I didn't. You can't get lost in a tunnel! I just went on alone and was taking pictures of the wall paintings. And then I remembered that the next train would be coming soon."

"And probably at about the same time, I looked around for Zoe, but didn't see her and started to get really worried ..." explained Basti.

"Yeah, you can say that again!" added Rick. "He was running around like a madman."

"And then what happened?" Debbie was both glad and sorry that she had missed all the excitement.

"Well, I dropped my spray can and started running after Basti. I caught up with him and tried to calm him down. Just in time we found these storage rooms off to the side of the tracks. I think homeless people sometimes live in them. We went into the first room, but no sign of Zoe and then a second one – and that's where we found the runaway."

"Wait a second," said Zoe, "there's more to this story. They didn't even see me at first. They saw somebody else."

"Mr. Kaminski," said Basti.

"Mr. Kaminski?" Debbie didn't understand.

"That's right – a really strange old guy," said Rick.

"I think he was sweet."

"Well, maybe to you, Zoe," said Rick.

"And this little room, which he calls his office, is full of old maps," added Basti.

"He also speaks with a funny accent. He sounds Russian or Polish, or something like that. And he told us that everybody down there knows him as the 'Professor'. He also gave Basti and me a hard time. He told us that we shouldn't have let Zoe out of our sight and that it is too dangerous down there for a girl to walk alone."

"I thought he was a really funny guy. He told us to come and visit him next time we are down there," said Basti.

"Well anyway," said Rick, "I'm hungry! What did you bring for us to eat?"

"I brought a lot," said Debbie, "I also brought a blanket so we can sit on the grass. Come on. Let's go over there." Debbie picked up the backpack and they all stepped over a very a small fence onto the thick green grass beyond.

☆

"What are you doing?" asked Basti.

"Oh, I'm just thinking about that graffiti I started in the Freedom Tunnel," said Rick, who was sitting on the floor in his room with ten or more street stickers around him. "I'd really like to go back and finish it … soon."

"Yeah, I'd like to go back there, too."

"Really? You know, I was thinking, Basti, that you and I could go alone – I mean without Moog and Raul – maybe even tomorrow."

"Tomorrow?"

"If I wait too long, somebody else is going to use that spot. They might even paint over what I've done so far," explained Rick. "We could go at the same time as before: between ten and ten thirty. We let a train pass and then run in!"

"How about Zoe?"

"Zoe? Do you think she'd want to come again? I think she had enough last time – I mean the whole thing with the trains must have scared the pants off her, don't you think? Anyway, she could also do something with Debbie."

"Yeah, I guess so … but maybe …" said Basti slowly.

"What?" asked Rick. He absolutely did not want to make the trip as complicated as last time.

"I'd just like to tell her, and if she really wants to come along …"

"We don't have to do everything together, you know. But, OK, if you want we can go ask them now."

☆

"No, I really don't want to go," said Debbie. "Tomorrow is supposed to be a really hot day and I was thinking that we could all go to Coney Island or Brighton Beach and swim in the ocean."

"Well, today's just Tuesday. You both could go to Brighton Beach tomorrow and we can all go to Coney Island on Thursday," suggested Rick. Basti stood in the doorway and Zoe sat quietly on her bed.

"You decided last time, Rick! Anyway, they've already been to the tunnel once! This time it's my turn to plan the day!" said Debbie excitedly. Her face and neck were turning red all the way to the roots of her hair that was pulled back in a ponytail.

"Shh! You don't have to scream. They can hear us," said Rick in a loud whisper.

"Don't tell me what to do! I can speak loudly if I want to!"

At that moment Uncle Ben entered the room. "Hey, what's this all about?"

Debbie quickly wiggled up from the bed to speak first.

"Dad, it's going to be very hot tomorrow and I think we should go to Coney Island, but Rick is insisting that we should all go to Riverside Park again and …"

"Yeah, Dad, it has the greatest skateboard park in the city and I wanted to show Basti … and then we could walk across the George Washington Bridge to Palisades Park, which is also on mom's list."

"But he decided last time and now it's my turn and anyway, he's lying!"

"Lying about what? What are you talking about?! And anyway, we're fine if Zoe and Debbie want to go to the beach tomorrow … Then Basti and I will go to the park alone."

"Come on you two – I think that's enough. Zoe and Basti are your guests, I think they should decide. Well, Zoe, it looks like it's up to you. What would you like to do?"

"I'm fine with both, but I would really like it if we all went together."

"How about you, Basti?"

"Both places are fine with me, too."

"Well, why don't we check the weather report for the rest of the week. On the hottest day you all go to the beach, I mean Coney Island, and on the other two days you can do other things. OK? But, you stay together."

☆

"Sorry, Rick," said Uncle Ben, as he returned to Debbie's room, "tomorrow, sunny and hot, 95°F; Thursday and Friday, partly cloudy, 87°F. I guess it's Debbie's call this time."

"Yeah, great, that's really great," said Rick sarcastically. "The four of us and half of New York are going to the beach tomorrow. I'm going out now, for a walk, alone!" Rick got up and made for the door. Uncle Ben grabbed his arm.

"Listen Rick," he said, "dinner will be ready in fifteen minutes – and before that, I'd like to talk to you. Let's go into my room for a moment. Debbie, Zoe and Basti, why don't you all go into the kitchen and see if Marion could use some help with dinner. We'll be eating on the balcony tonight, so I'm sure there are a lot of things to take out."

"Sure, Dad," said Debbie.

"Come on, Rick, come with me."

☆

When the Kranbacher and Meyer kids walked out the next morning from the air-conditioned lobby to the street, the heavy hot air seemed to take their breath away. Their backpacks, each packed with a beach towel, sun cream and part of the picnic lunch suddenly felt heavier. It took a lot of energy to walk and keep their eyes from closing in the muggy air.

"Wow! This is the hottest weather I've ever been in," said Zoe, taking off her light sweatshirt and tying it around her waist.

"You can say that again!" agreed Debbie.

"Yeah, maybe we should have stayed home," said Rick who was still angry not to be going to the tunnel today.

"I think this is a perfect day for the beach," said Debbie who was dressed head-to-toe in 'beach chic'. Her flip-flops had a pink plastic flower next to the big toe. She was wearing white short shorts with a pink chain belt and a bright yellow halter top. She also had on extra large sunglasses and her frizzy blond hair was tied back in a ponytail by another pink plastic flower. Zoe pretended to be a fashion photographer, and asked Debbie to pose on the promenade with the Hudson River and the Statue of Liberty in the background while she took photos of her. She also made a series of close-ups just of Debbie's face. Rick and Basti came over.

"Hey, let me see those," Rick said, almost grabbing the camera out of Zoe's hands.

"This a great photo of you, Debbie," said Rick, laughing at one of the close-up shots. "I think you can get a lead role in one of those insect movies! You can call yourself Bug-Face Meyer!" It was true – those huge glasses made her look insect-like, especially with her hair pulled back so tight.

Still, Zoe didn't find it funny at all. She took the camera out of Rick's hand and gave Basti a long, angry look. "Come on, Debbie. Let's go." Debbie started walking without saying anything to her brother. She was happy to be going to the beach with Zoe on her side.

At the Broadway – Nassau Street Station they caught the A train to Brooklyn and then changed to an F train to Coney Island. They had to take this train to the last stop on the line – 40 minutes! The train was almost empty. Debbie and Zoe sat on one side, while Rick and Basti stretched out on the empty seats opposite. Debbie gave the others pieces of soft pink bubblegum and they all spent the next ten minutes in competition over who could blow the biggest bubble.

Bubble after bubble, it was clear that Debbie was the bubblegum queen. A few times you could hardly see her face behind her pink creations. That is, until one of her largest bubbles floated upwards – and popped leaving sticky pink stuff all over Debbie's shiny sunglasses. "Uh-oh," said Zoe. Rick laughed out loud and slapped Basti on the back. The sudden hit made Basti swallow his gum. Rick kept on laughing as if Debbie's bubble blowing misadventure were the funniest thing he had ever seen. Debbie looked back at him angrily. She took off her glasses and after peeling off the thin pink film from her lips, she started to get the stuff off her brand new glasses. Zoe found an old tissue in the front pocket of her backpack and discreetly removed the ball of gum from her mouth. Rick was still laughing, rocking back and forth in his seat and slapping his leg. What he didn't notice: his bubblegum had fallen out of his open mouth and landed on his leg. Rick let his hand come right down on the sticky piece of gum. Basti thought this was very funny and finally started laughing. Rick was now silent. He got up, went over to Zoe and quietly asked her if she had another tissue. Zoe pulled out a whole pack and the bubblegum bubble blowing competition was now officially over.

"Hey guys, we get off at the next stop," said Debbie, still fighting with the pink bubblegum on her sunglasses.

"No rush," said Rick. "Stillwell Avenue is the last stop on the line."

Debbie slipped her sunglasses into her bag and pulled out a pink sun hat. It seemed as if everybody on that train was going to the same place. People were carrying beach chairs, balls, and picnic coolers and, like Debbie, were wearing flip-flops and sun hats.

☆

Even when Zoe was still on the subway platform, her nose picked up a new smell: it was the salty air of the sea. Manhattan's smell was different – there the streets smelled of bricks and concrete, dirt and cars. They walked along Surf Avenue. Here most of the buildings weren't buildings at all, not floor above floor above floor, no regular windows, no towers of shiny glass and steel facades. In Coney Island the low buildings were made of signs: big signs, little signs and cartoon-like pictures. All the signs welcomed people in for 'Ice Cold Drinks and the Juiciest Burgers', for the 'Freshest Seafood' or for the 'Ride of Your Life'. Every sign celebrated an experience. And then there was the beach: the place where the city ends.

Even before they reached the beach promenade, Zoe had the feeling that she could see more of the sky here. She looked through the eye of her camera: Yes, more sky … in fact she even felt she could look over the top of the buildings. This place was so different from New York City. Left and right there were small buildings, but straight ahead it was totally open: the Atlantic Ocean. Sail across and they'd be back in Germany. But there was something else. Here in Coney Island it looked as if people were getting ready for a big party or a fair. The signs, the bright colors, the old-fashioned lights and the smells of candied peanuts, popcorn, cotton candy and sausages and hot dogs made this feeling even stronger. And what would happen on a very stormy day, she wondered. Could huge waves rush up Surf Avenue all the way to the subway station? Would the strong wind blow against the low buildings and large signs? Would the chairs and tables outside the restaurants and snack bars just be blown away?

They walked down Statton Avenue to the beach. Zoe noticed that if she looked one way through her camera, she saw the Parachute Jump and if she looked the other way a huge ferris wheel appeared behind the low buildings.

"Hey Zoe, with that thing in front of your face all the time, you're starting to look like a filmmaker … *German Director films new Blockbuster movie on location: 'The Coney Island*

Killers' stars budding new actress Debbie 'Bug face' Meyer ..." Zoe lowered her camera. She was getting tired of Rick's nasty comments. Without looking at him, she ran up to Debbie and whispered something in her ear.

The street ended in the promenade and they started running. The beach side promenade, which Rick and Debbie called 'the Boardwalk', was made of thin wood boards and was raised about eight feet above the sand. It went on as far as one could see. Although it was only 10 o'clock, the beach was already full of people.

"Let's go on," said Debbie, "maybe there will be fewer people up ahead." They walked on in silence listening to little kids shouting to their mothers and mothers shouting back to their kids. They heard the far away sound of waves slapping against the sandy shore, but most of all, they heard the sound of Debbie's beach sandals. Her flip-flops slapping against the bouncy wood boards of the boardwalk was like the rhythm section in a band. And it was not long before Rick started rapping to the slapping sound of her shoes. It went like this:

"Flip-Flop, Flip-Flop
They don't stop
flippin', floppin'
Talkin' while they're walkin'
Flippin' Floppin'
Boardwalk talkin'

She's a Bug face Beauty,
Bubblegum queen
She's got a cool dude brother,
but he's real mean –

Flippin', floppin'
Talkin' while they're walkin'
Flippin', floppin'
Boardwalk walkin'

Then they walked down some steps to the beach below and Rick changed the words to his song:

Sinkin' in the sand
Sinkin' in the sand
flip-flops flippin' floppin'
Sinkin' in the sand.

Debbie slipped off her sandals and, turning to Rick, smiled and kept on walking towards an emptier spot.

"This looks good," she said, dropping her backpack. There was a kissing pair a few meters away and another group of teenagers behind them playing cards on a large blanket. At least there was enough room to lay down their towels, but not much else. The waves looked great – high enough to body surf but slowly uncurling before slapping against the sand. Zoe ran towards the water. Rick pretended to fall and let himself be knocked down by the next wave. Zoe turned back to look towards their towels. "Come on in, Debbie," she shouted.

☆

The sun was high up in the sky and more people were arriving, which meant more beach chairs, picnic coolers, more children and more oiled bodies lying in the sun.

Just then a family of five came towards them waddling across the sand like ducks. They set up their things a few feet away. Not only was one of their three kids a crying baby, they had also brought a huge radio, which was playing loud music. The father stuck a very large beach umbrella into the ground and set up two beach chairs: one for himself and one for his gigantic wife. Before another minute went by, she had opened up their red and white picnic box and started handing out food to her children.

"Uh-oh," said Basti quietly.

"Yup, I think it's time to pack up and head over to the *Cyclone* or to the *El Dorado Bumper Car Arcade*. What do you say, 'Bug-Face'?" asked Rick.

"Rick, if you call me that one more time, I'm going to tell Mom and Dad that you went to the Freedom Tunnel with Basti and Zoe. Got that?" Rick didn't answer.

"I asked you a question, Rick," said Debbie in a very serious tone.

"Yes," he said finally.

"OK, good. By the way, where's Zoe?" said Debbie shaking off sand from her arms and legs.

"She's over there taking photographs."

"OK, let's get going."

They packed up everything and crossed the beach to pick up Zoe. They found her by the boardwalk where she was trying to capture the rays of sunlight shooting through the boards to the cool, dark sand below. Debbie, Rick and Basti stood quietly until she had finished her shot. Zoe stood up.

"We're going to the *El Dorado Bumper Car Arcade*." Basti handed her her backpack and they all climbed back up to the boardwalk.

☆

It was around 4 pm when they went back towards the train station. Debbie had no more gum and was hurting from a sunburn on her neck and shoulders and the back of her legs. Zoe was reviewing all the photos she had taken that day. Basti and Rick quickly fell asleep to the subway train's gentle rocking.

Chapter 5

"You know those photos I took of you yesterday on the promenade with the river behind you?" Debbie nodded as she turned a page.

"Well some of them came out pretty well. I was thinking that we could take more like that in the tunnel tomorrow. It would be like a fashion shoot."

"A fashion shoot?" Debbie turned away from her magazine to look straight at Zoe.

"Yeah, we'll think about what you can wear ... and I'll start thinking of where I could get the best shots."

"What *can* I wear?"

"Well, it's pretty dark down there. But light comes down from above in some places. So I was thinking that you could wear very bright, colorful clothes. You know, something like what you wore to the beach – yellow would be good, or bright red. Where the light comes down the bright colors will shine. And in the shadows, the color will be there too, just darker ... And I think your hair should be out."

"You mean like this?" Debbie slipped the hair band off and shaped her hair by squeezing it in her bony hands. "And make-up? How about make-up?" she asked, clearly starting to get excited, "I have a lot here: dark black eyeliner, purple or gold eyeshadow, lip gloss and lipstick."

"Hmm ... that's a good idea ... make-up would be good, especially the eyeliner, but I think if you wear something on your lips it shouldn't be too shiny. The photos will be about color in dark places – you know where you see it and where you don't. I'm going to photograph you half in the dark and half in light, and your light blond hair is perfect for that."

"Wow, Zoe, you sound like an artist! That's a really cool idea. I could try on the clothes and make-up now. Let me show you the clothes I've got …"

☆

"So we're all going tomorrow – I didn't expect it, but that's cool," said Rick shaking each spray can in his black bag.

"This one's empty." He held up a can of white paint and shook it up and down a few times. It made a loud rattling sound. "Yup, empty." He pulled out a new can with a white cap from a shopping bag and put it in the black bag. "I'm going to be totally ready when I go down there tomorrow."

"How about you, Basti? Do you have any special plans for tomorrow? You could make your own mark in the tunnel. I could teach you some techniques."

"Well, I don't have any special name. I don't know what I would write. I'm happy to help you," said Basti, picking up one of the empty cans and holding it close to his ear as he gave it a good shake.

"Sure," said Rick, "but I thought you might want to do something of your own."

"Actually, I was planning to visit Mr. Kaminski again."

"Yeah, really? Why do you want to do that? That old guy talks too much."

"But he's got some great old maps and … it's hard to explain … I'd just like to check him out again …"

"Yeah, well, if that's what you want to do, it's fine with me. You don't have to explain anything. For me that tunnel is about graffiti – underground art."

☆

The next morning, Debbie and Zoe woke up at 7:30 am. They had a lot to do to get ready. Debbie's clothes were all carefully laid out on her desk chair. The night before they had chosen a bright yellow armless dress, red capri pants and long, red satin gloves that she had secretly borrowed from her mother. They ate breakfast in their pajamas and returned to Debbie's room to dress and put on the make-up. Debbie outlined her brown eyes with a fine black line and brushed her lids with purple eyeshadow. With a lip pencil she had found in the bathroom cabinet she drew a line at the edge of her top and bottom lips. The only question was – what shoes would Debbie wear? For climbing over the fence and walking in the tunnel sneakers would be best, but sneakers wouldn't fit with the rest of her clothes.

"Let's pack these," said Zoe, pointing to a pair of red leather sandals, "you can put them on just for the shoot."

☆

They headed towards the subway station, each with his or her own thoughts about the trip. Zoe walked next to Debbie, sometimes stepping behind her or walking sideways to see her in profile. All this was preparation for photographing her later on. Debbie was concentrating on her walk. She felt like a model about to walk down the 'catwalk' in front of all the lights and cameras. In his mind, Rick painted 'The BORG 2009' and his signature figure over and over. He thought about how he could end a line perfectly and how to control the spray so there would be no drips. Basti realized that he would be visiting Mr. Kaminski alone this time. And what if the 'Professor' was not in his office? Well, he could always explore more of the tunnel.

When they took the path to Freedom Tunnel, it felt as if they had made this trip many times before.

At the tunnel entrance they all checked their watches. "We've got about eight minutes," said Zoe. She turned to

Debbie. "The trains come every 40 minutes. You don't have to worry, I'll make sure we are in a safe place when a train goes by."

Debbie looked confused, but she just nodded.

"How long are we going to stay? Maybe we should make a meeting place," suggested Basti.

"Good idea, bro," said Rick. "I think I need at least an hour to finish my work. Why don't you guys come and get me after the third train passes. Let's see, the first train will come at 11:05, then 11:45 and then 12:25. So I guess that means we all meet at about 12:45. OK?"

"OK," agreed Zoe and Basti.

"Here it comes!" said Basti. He was facing the tunnel entrance and could see the train's headlight, coming closer very fast. Zoe grabbed Debbie's arm and pulled her onto the dirty grass sprouting up beside the tracks. They heard the loud horn as the train flew by, rattling the tracks and blowing the smell of machine oil into their faces.

"OK, let's go!" shouted Rick running towards the tunnel entrance. Zoe took one last look and taking Debbie's hand followed Rick into the tunnel. They walked as a group – deeper into the tunnel. It was quiet enough that they could hear the shouts of children playing in the park above their heads. Debbie had her eyes on the ground. She was trying to be extra careful not to step on any garbage. Up ahead Zoe could see the sunlight coming from openings in the tunnel roof. She kept her eye on Debbie as she walked through the light and then back into the darkness. They reached the spot where Rick had started his artwork.

"Phew! What a relief! It's just as I left it," he said, dropping his black bag underneath the big 'B'. "OK guys, this is my spot. Just come back when you're finished. I'll be here hip-hoppin' and spraying my tag! *Bis bald!*" Rick pulled out the new can of black paint and started shaking the can as if it were a musical instrument.

The others kept on walking. It was not long before they reached one of the beautiful paintings that was right under the light. The painting was of a face, a woman's or a young boy's face, it was hard to tell.

"This is where I want to take the first photos, Debbie. Go up and touch the cheek," said Zoe.

"The cheek? You want me to touch the wall?"

"That's right. Put your hand on that cheek, right below the eye." Debbie did as she was told and Zoe started shooting photos.

"Now, keep your hand on the face and turn towards me. Yes, that's great! OK, just one more. Good! OK, now I want you to go on the other side of the face. The painting is in profile and I want you to also be in profile. Yes, that's right – I only want to see one side of your face. Wait a second. Move a little closer. Your nose should almost be touching her nose. Beautiful! Got it."

Basti looked on in surprise. His sister sounded like a professional photographer. When did that happen? he asked himself. She had only gotten that camera a few months ago. "Are you guys going to stay here for a while?" he asked.

"No we're finished here. There are some other great backgrounds I'd like to use. Hold on ... I think I'd like to take some shots of Debbie standing on the tracks. See that light coming down straight through the darkness? That would be perfect." Zoe was pointing to a spot about 10 meters further down. Debbie still looked a bit confused but she followed Zoe's lead. Her cousin's excitement was catchy.

"OK, then, I'm going to go ahead," said Basti, but Zoe barely heard him, she was too busy planning the next shot.

"Oops!" she said. "We forgot to change your shoes! It would be great if you were wearing the sandals when you stand on the tracks. Your feet will definitely be in this picture."

"Are you sure it's safe to stand on the metal?" asked Debbie feeling a bit nervous.

"Well, look, we've still got another 25 minutes before the next train comes. In 15 minutes, we'll go off to the side where it is totally safe. OK with you?"

"Yeah, I guess so. This whole place is pretty scary though," said Debbie.

"I'm going to go on," said Basti a little louder. "If you need me, I'll be with the Professor – you remember where he is, right Zoe?"

"You mean Mr. Kaminski?"

"That's right."

"Yes, I remember. We might stop by later."

"OK, *tschüs.*"

"Ciao," said Zoe. "OK, Debbie, let's get going. I don't want to miss that great light."

Debbie slipped her other shoes out of her bag. In the dirty, dark tunnel, the red sandals looked like the elegant evening shoes of an actress. With the fancy clothes she was wearing, and especially the long red satin evening gloves, Debbie felt like a movie star in an adventure film. This was the part in the movie when she and her tough partner had to run through a dark, damp underground tunnel to escape the bad guy who is after them.

Zoe looked over at Debbie, who was trying not to let her bare toes touch the ground as she changed shoes. Zoe rushed over and offered her arm for support. Debbie still wobbled a bit on one leg. They both started laughing.

"Ready?" asked Zoe.

"I'm as ready as I'll ever be!"

"OK, let's get to work. Can you please stand with those fancy red slippers directly on the tracks?"

"With both feet?"

"Yes, if that's possible."

"I'll try. There isn't much space to stand ... How's this?"

"Good, good. But can you stay still in that position?"

"Y-ee-ss, I thi-ink so."

"Now hold on, I want you to move a bit to the left. In this shot, only half of your body will be in the light."

"Like this?"

"Yes! Great! Now, just hold it!" Zoe took picture after picture. "That was perfect!"

The light was streaming in from above cutting across Debbie's figure. On that side, her blond hair, and the yellow dress looked as if they were glowing in the darkness.

"I've got another idea, Debbie. Can you get on your knees and put your hands on the track in front of you? Yes, just like that. Now just go forward a bit along the track. I just want your face and shoulders to be in the light – as if you're coming out of the darkness. Okaaaay ... great!"

"Zoe?"

"Just a second ... I just want to get this shot." Debbie was looking out of the corner of her eye at Zoe's watch. It was hard to tell from down where she was, but it looked like Zoe's watch read 11:42.

"Zoe, I think you should check the time ..."

"Time? Oh right – the time. Oh my God! You're right – the train will be coming in a few minutes." Zoe stood up straight and looked around for a safe place to go. "We've got to get over to the side there. Can you pick up your things fast – I've got to get my bag. It's next to the other track."

"Zoe! Where are my sneakers?" shouted Debbie. "Are they over there?"

"No!" Zoe shouted back. "Come on, we don't have any more time to look. Just come ... follow me! We have to move faster!" Zoe started running towards a niche in the wall. Debbie couldn't keep up with her. The heels of her sandals kept getting caught between the stones.

"I can't run in these shoes!" Debbie was almost in tears.

"Let me help you. Just take my hand. But we have to move quickly ... This way." Zoe almost pushed Debbie against the wall. It was just wide enough for the two of them. Zoe turned her head – there was the bright yellow shine of the train's headlight ... then the loud horn. She took a deep breath: safe, again. But just in time! The silver train cars rattled by. Zoe felt for Debbie's hand and squeezed it tight until the train disappeared into the distance.

At first, Zoe couldn't look Debbie in the face. She was too ashamed. She should have paid better attention to the time. For a good photograph, she had risked Debbie's safety. "I'm really sorry," she managed to say. "That was so stupid of me not to check the time."

"Yeah, well, we made it. That's the important thing. But I want to go and see if my sneakers came through all right."

"Oh, right – your sneakers." Zoe looked around and spotted a white sneaker between two wood boards. "Here's one," she said, holding the still white sneaker up in the air for Debbie to see.

"And here's the other," said Debbie.

"Wow, it looks like the train ran right over your sneaker! I wonder if a small object like that can cause an accident!"

"I don't know. All I know is that I have one white and one black and white sneaker."

"I'm sorry, Debbie! I promise I'll get you another pair."

"Come on, it's OK. When we get home tonight these are definitely going in the wash and then we'll see. Don't worry about it. We're in this one together." Debbie went over and hugged Zoe.

"You know what, Zoe ... dangerous or not, this is exciting. Right? So what's next? How much time do we have until the next train comes?" Zoe looked at her watch. It was 11:58.

"About 20 minutes."

"That's not much time to do another shoot is it?"

"Not really. But we could go and visit Mr. Kaminski. That's where Basti is. I think you should meet him. He's quite a character. And anyway, in his office we'll be safe when the next train comes."

"Sounds good to me." As if following a cue, Zoe and Debbie did their own version of a soul shake.

☆

Basti whistled as he walked deeper into the tunnel. He was alone now, on his way to Mr. Kaminski's office. The whistling was helping him remember something. Something from a long time ago. It had to do with another old man in his life – his grandfather. That was it, his grandfather always whistled. Basti looked up. Splashes of color flashed at him from the tunnel walls. He looked to the right and to the left – more and more graffiti. The graffiti were the traces of all the people who had been here. Every ten steps he walked into the light coming from above. The light hit his head like a short shower, a short warm shower. He passed a wall painting which he recognized. And there was Mr. Kaminski's door: the few steps leading to the door and the hand-painted 'Home Sweet Home'. Basti knocked.

"*Komm rein,*" a voice answered. German! Basti couldn't believe his ears. Slowly and carefully he opened the door. Mr. Kaminski was sitting behind his old metal desk just like the last time.

"Good to see you, my boy. I was wondering when you would come by again. Come over here, I want to show you something. I think you'll find it interesting."

On his desk were several photographs of an old building. It looked like a Greek or Roman temple full of light. In one picture the light came through high arching windows, and in another it came through a glass roof.

"This, my dear boy, is the old Pennsylvania Station: New York 1910 to 1963. Before I tell you about this building, I want to tell you a little story about myself.

"I come from a very big family," said Mr. Kaminski. "Believe it or not, I had four sisters and two and a half brothers and then me. I was second to last. There was Berta, Sam, Murray, Jimmy (he was the half), Edith, Shari and Ruth," explained Mr. Kaminski, counting each kid on the fingers of his hand. "We didn't have a lot of money in those days, but we had each other. One of us was always making the rest of us laugh. That was usually my brother Sammy – he was a comedian – and my sister Shari. They knew how to put on a show! We were a loud and funny family ... and always busy. Sometimes it was too much for me. So I escaped, here to this station – Penn Station. I really had nowhere else to go. As a boy I loved the trains. I'd take the subway – it cost only 5 cents in those days – and ride up to Penn Station ... you know as if I was going someplace. Truth was, I had no place to go. I had no uncle in Albany or cousins in Boston or upstate in Buffalo. I just went to the station because for me as a boy it was the most exciting place to be.

"Then wouldn't you know, my first job is right there – in Pennsylvania Station and I'm not talking about that horrible rat box they call Penn Station today. I mean the old Station, the most beautiful building this city has ever had. Boy, it was a palace – grand staircases, sky-high roof, all glass, huge windows and gloriously tiled floors.

Yes, sir, when I was 17, I became a track man. It was our job to make sure that the tracks out in the tunnels were just as they should be. It was hard work – but I never minded. Just to see the light coming through those high windows … it was heaven. Then the big men at the top decided to tear the old station down."

"Why?" asked Basti, looking at an old photograph of Pennsylvania Station's waiting room.

"My boy, some things in life are very simple. There was only one reason that they decided to replace the old station with this modern garbage: money! Money, money, and more money ... for those idiots who don't understand anything about a great city, great architecture and trains. They just did a little 1+1 ... child's maths. Look, if you put one office floor on top of another until you have 45 floors of offices and each office pays rent, well, somebody is going to make a lot of money. Penn Station took up a lot of land in midtown New York. They built an office tower, the station, and a sports complex called 'Madison Square Garden'. A small group of people could make a lot of money, my boy, that's why they tore down one of the world's most beautiful stations 53 years after it was built! It makes my blood boil! I'm sorry, Sebastian, that I can't show you where I worked for the ten happiest years of my life but I can at least show you these fine pictures of the old days – some glorious earlier days! And I can tell you," said Mr. Kaminski, pressing his finger into Basti's chest, "yes, where you can find some relics of the Grand Old Penn Station." Basti looked confused.

"I bet you don't know what a relic is."

Basti shook his head.

"Well, let me tell you. A relic or an artefact is something old which is left behind when somebody dies or something is destroyed. That means that the old is never completely replaced with the new. Even though we call this crazy city 'New York', there are some old treasures here for the curious."

Chapter 6

Mr. Kaminski suddenly spoke very softly. He leaned forward and just about whispered in Basti's ear as though he were about to tell him a secret. "I can tell you where you can find a few parts of the old station in the new one. What do you say, my boy, are you ready to do a little exploring?"

"Yes! Please tell me."

"You see this eagle? In this picture, they're bringing this proud stone bird down from its place on the top edge of the station entrance. These criminals tore down the whole building but kept the eagles. They probably knew that they could sell them at a good price. Anyway, now these eagles are all over the country. Only one is still there keeping guard outside the 7th Avenue entrance of Penn Station ... I'm going to write that down for you." Mr. Kaminski took out a yellowing piece of paper from his shirt pocket and unfolded it. He wrote down the following: '1. Eagle; location: 7th Avenue between 33rd and 34th Streets'.

"OK then. Now let's go inside. This, Basti, is the entrance hall. You used to come from the street and walk down these marble steps. You'd buy a ticket and then walk into a light-filled space. You'd look up at the timetable board to find the right platform and go down the stairs. The light would follow you down. Now, if you go to Penn Station today, you can only find one of the original staircases. It goes to platform 5 and 6 of the New Jersey Transit. I have no idea why they saved one staircase, but it's there. So that's the second relic. And I'm going to write that down, too." Mr. Kaminski picked up his soft pencil and carefully wrote '2. Original staircase; location: 'platform 5 and 6, NJ transit'.

Mr. Kaminski went on to describe three other locations in the new station. "There you go, my boy. Here is the list. See how many you can find." Mr. Kaminski started folding up the paper along the same creases just like one does with a well-used map and was about to hand it to Basti when there was a sudden knock on the door.

"Did you hear that?" asked Mr. Kaminski.

"What?" said Basti.

"That knocking sound. Listen. There it is again. Someone must be at the door. Go and take a look, my boy." Basti got up and when he opened the door, there stood Zoe and Debbie, politely waiting to be invited into Mr. Kaminski's office. One of Zoe's bare shoulders was black with dirt and Debbie had a big black smudge across her forehead in addition to the make-up that she had put on in the morning.

"Now there's a sight for sore eyes!" exclaimed Mr. Kaminski. "Come in, come in. Marvelous to see you, young lady. And who, might I ask, are you?"

"This is Debbie, our other cousin. She's Rick's younger sister."

"Welcome, Debbie. My name is Kaminski, Leo Kaminski, former track man, now resident professor, Freedom Tunnel, New York." The way Mr. Kaminski was carrying on, Zoe was almost expecting him to salute to the two of them. Instead he just said, "Come and make yourselves comfortable. Have a seat." Unfortunately, there were only two chairs in Mr. Kaminski's office and the Professor was already sitting in one of them. Basti stood up and offered his chair to Debbie and Zoe. They each sat on one corner while Basti stood at one side of the large desk.

"I was just telling Basti about the old Penn Station – the cathedral of transportation. But tell me, what has my favorite German tourist been up to since her last visit?"

"We've been to Central Park and Coney Island."

"Coney Island – New York's fantasy land. I remember jumping off the Parachute Tower with my sweetheart Rachel Stein. We held hands all the way down. When we got down to the bottom, I asked her to marry me. That was back in 1952 and I had just turned seventeen. Of course she was only fifteen and asked me to wait a few years … I guess they've closed that old thing …"

Zoe and Debbie looked at one another and laughed. Still the thought of jumping with your boyfriend a distance of 200 feet sounded pretty exciting.

"Can I take a picture of you, Mr. Kaminski?" asked Zoe.

"I don't see why not … as long as you're not with the FBI. In fact I would be honored." Zoe took several shots of Mr. Kaminski. After a few typical portraits, she asked him to spread out a map on the table. He chose a map of the tracks leaving Penn Station and then he pointed to the track which led to the Freedom Tunnel. He looked up at the kids and Zoe snapped a shot.

"And how about a picture of Basti and me – veterans of the NY Underground?" Zoe nodded and Basti went over to stand beside Mr. Kaminski. The old man put his arm around Basti. As he lifted his arm, Zoe could see that there were several holes in his light brown sweater.

"How about one of us all together?" asked Mr. Kaminski.

"Sure, I can do that. I just need to find a good place for the camera and then I can set the timer." Zoe put her camera on top of one of the boxes which held the maps. She pressed a button and slipped over to join the others. "OK, we have thirty seconds."

"Say cheese," said Debbie. The camera made a buzzing sound and it was over. Debbie lifted Zoe's wrist to check the time. "It's 12:15, shouldn't we go back to Rick soon?" she whispered.

"We still have about 15 minutes," Zoe whispered back.

Mr. Kaminski looked over to Debbie. "Do you know, you remind me of my little sister Ruth – she was eight years younger than me and had blond fluffy hair just like you. There was one thing that Ruth loved, and that was hot dogs. She was thin like you, but she could eat about four hot dogs in next to no time. Speaking of Coney Island ... Did you try the frankfurters at Nathan's?" Debbie and Zoe looked at each other again, smiled and nodded their heads.

"As we're on the subject of my family ... Ruth was the youngest, and as I was telling your brother, there were eight of us. We all lived on the Lower East Side." Mr. Kaminski opened a large map of Manhattan that covered his table. Basti quickly pointed to Battery Park City – the piece of land that sticks out into the Hudson River on the west side of Manhattan Island.

"This is where our cousins live," said Basti.

"Oh-ho! That's a fancy address, right on the river. Well then, let's start at your cousins' place and I'll walk you to my old neighborhood. Here, we'll start by walking up Liberty Street to Broadway. We'll then go up Broadway to Park Row and go around City Hall – Brooklyn Bridge is off to the right, but we just keep on walking straight. Park Row becomes Center Street and we go up Center Street and walk straight through good old Chinatown. We cross Canal Street and take our next right. See here – that's Hester Street. We walk down Hester Street and once we cross the Bowery, we've made it to the Lower East Side. Just a few more blocks east and there's Orchard Street – the heart of the old neighborhood. You could walk down Orchard Street and believe you were in Krakow, Lodz or Prague: it was home away from home. Orchard Street was the shopping center – shop after shop. We had men's clothes, women's clothes, shops for the little ones, delicatessens with food from every part of Europe – Sauergurken, Roggenbrot, Lachs, Herring, and Bagels ... you name it, we got it. You could find everything on Orchard Street and at a very good price, too. My father, his name was Josef, but everybody called him Joe – he and his brothers Michael and Max, had a haberdashery, you know, they sold hats. *Kaminski's Hats* was the name. *Kaminski's* had men's hats: bowlers, Stetsons, hats for the older and religious men – the serious hats we called them – and then chic hats for the ladies. All three families lived above the shop at 131 Orchard Street. Uncle Michael's family lived on the second floor, we lived on the third floor and Uncle Max's family lived under the roof. My mother had a little workshop in the back and whenever a lady walked into the shop, Pop would call her out. 'Sharon!' he'd call out, and she would come out smiling. My mother knew exactly which hat would look the best. She'd take one look at the lady, pretend to think hard and choose what she knew to be the right hat for the face. The ladies would walk around the shop thinking they looked like a movie star – Marlene Dietrich or Marilyn Monroe and Pop would wink at my mother. He always said she was the best business partner a man could wish for.

In the summertime," said Mr. Kaminski, "when it got too hot in our apartment, we would climb out the windows and sit on the fire escapes. Fire escapes were just stuck onto the outside of every building in those days for a quick escape in case of fire. I could sit out there for hours just watching the life on the street below."

"Do you still live on Orchard Street, Mr. Kaminski?" asked Basti.

"I haven't been down there for years!" said Mr. Kaminski throwing up his hands. "I live uptown now ... and I spend so much time in the office, you could almost say that I live here ... hah!"

"And what happened to *Kaminski's Hats*?" said Zoe, hoping for more stories.

"Well, my father and his brothers passed away many years ago. My brother Max and my mother ran the shop together. But when my mother died, Max sold the place. That must have been about 15 years ago. He lives out in Jersey now. Actually, Shari is the only one of us who stayed in the old neighborhood. She worked in a children's hospital, but she's retired now."

Just then a train went by.

"That must be the 12:25 to Albany. Hah! It's only one minute late! That's a new record."

"I guess we'd better get going, Mr. Kaminski. We told Rick we'd pick him up in about twenty minutes."

"Well, then don't forget these," said Mr. Kaminski and put the photo of the stone eagle and the glass-covered entrance hall of Penn Station and the list of relics that he had written up into Basti hands. "These photos might be helpful for your explorations," he said winking at Basti. "I'm sorry I don't have anything for these young ladies. I'll have to ask my sister Shari if she has any of the old hats packed away somewhere in her wardrobe. Those hats would look great on these two beauties. Next time I'll have them for you."

☆

Basti went up close to the wall and put his finger to the black paint.

"Still wet," he said, "so he couldn't have left that long ago."

"What time is it?" asked Debbie.

"Ten to one," said Zoe. "We're only a few minutes late."

"I don't understand. Why would he leave? It's not like him."

"Waaah!" screamed Rick jumping out of the shadows. "I was sitting here the whole time. I just wanted you to see my work on the wall without me sitting right in front."

Debbie went over and gave her brother a quick hug. "You know, for once in my life, I'm really happy to see you. I think I've had enough surprises for one day." Just then a pair of rats scurried along the wall right under Rick's graffiti.

"Oh my God, raaaaats!" screamed Debbie pointing to the two little bodies. Her words echoed through the tunnel and the rats disappeared.

"Well, you sure scared them away. I don't think they'll be coming back," said Rick, laughing.

Zoe looked at her watch. "I think we should get out of here, the next train is coming in five minutes." Debbie started sneezing.

"Yeah, let's go, the dirt is really starting to get to me."

"I think we're too late now. Let's just wait until this one passes," said Basti checking his watch.

"Come over here," said Rick leading the others to a dark area where the tunnel wall stepped back. They all stood close to one another. It was so quiet Zoe could hear her brother's breathing. A minute later the train raced by. Zoe looked at Basti, Debbie and Rick, their heads were only centimeters away. The train was gone and the Meyers and Kranbachers ran out of the tunnel into the bright hot day.

Chapter 7

The next morning, Basti and Zoe woke up early, washed and dressed and found themselves alone, together at the kitchen table. Uncle Ben and Aunt Marion had already left for work and Debbie and Rick were still fast asleep. In the middle of the kitchen table, leaning against the salt and pepper shakers, was a carefully written note. Basti got close to read it and then showed it to Zoe who was busy getting cereal bowls and cornflakes down from the kitchen cupboard.

"Did you see this?" asked Basti.

"No, what does it say?"

To Rick, Debbie, Zoe and Basti,
Please meet Ben and me at the Wong Fat Restaurant,
67 Mott Street at 6 pm.
Don't be late! Have a great day!
Love, Marion (Mom)

"*Wong Fat?* ... That's a strange name for a restaurant. Anyway, what should we do today?" said Zoe, putting a bowl and spoon in front of Basti.

"Mott Street – isn't that one of the streets Mr. Kaminski talked about? I think it might be in the neighborhood where he grew up. We could visit his street before going to the restaurant," Basti suggested.

"Yeah, we could do that, but that won't take all day ... What else is there?"

"How about the Brooklyn Bridge?" said Basti filling up his bowl with cornflakes. Zoe found the sugar bowl and put it down next to Basti's bowl. He spooned out two heaped teaspoons and then a third. Zoe got out the milk, set it on the table and finally sat down.

"Is it a long walk?" asked Zoe.

"Where?" said Basti, his mouth full of cornflakes.

"Across the Brooklyn Bridge, dummy."

"I'm not really sure," said Basti. "But Rick will know."

"Anyway, I think it's a good idea," said Zoe grabbing the cereal box to read while she ate.

The bathroom door slammed shut and a sleepy-looking Rick stumbled down the hallway towards the kitchen.

"Morning."

"Good morning," said Basti and Zoe in chorus.

"Is mom already gone?" Rick asked scratching his head and yawning.

"Yes, but she left this note. Here – " Basti passed the note to his cousin. Rick poured himself a large glass of orange juice. "Do you guys want some?"

Basti and Zoe shook their heads. Rick stretched open his eyes and read the note.

"We were thinking it might be a good day to see the Brooklyn Bridge," said Zoe.

"Sounds good, but I don't think I can make it. Moog called me last night. He and Raul want me to come over and work on some street stickers. I'm probably going to spend the day with them. I'm not sure what Debbie's up to, but maybe she can take you. I can't do it."

Just then Debbie appeared in the kitchen. "Good morning, everybody," she said.

"Hey Sis, what are you doing today?"

"Well, like always, I have my jazz dance class at 12 o'clock and then I'm going to meet Jocelyn. She just got back from a trip and she really wants to see me. She's been in Mexico for the past two weeks. Mom said it's OK. She said you could take Basti and Zoe somewhere today."

"Oh great – it's always me! I mean, nothing against you guys, but I've already told Moog that I'd be there," said Rick hitting his orange juice glass down hard on the kitchen counter. Debbie jumped back. "Hey Rick, what's wrong with you!? Calm down!"

"No problem," said Zoe. "Of course you should go! We'll be fine on our own."

"That would help me out a lot. I'd really like to join you guys but it's kind of important to get together with Moog and Raul, you know," said Rick.

"Hey, Rick, you don't have to take us everywhere. We'd be happy to explore the city by ourselves," added Basti.

Debbie grabbed a bowl from the cupboard and sat down next to Zoe. Zoe passed over the cornflakes, the milk, the sugar and then Aunt Marion's note.

"Oh cool – Chinatown! I love Chinese food! *Wong Fat* has the best fried noodles and Peking Duck."

"I was wondering, how long does it take to walk across the Brooklyn Bridge?" asked Zoe.

"Is that what you guys are planning to do?" asked Debbie.

"Oh, I guess it would take about half an hour," answered Rick. "But, wait a second, I've got a better idea – you can use our bikes and ride across. There is even a bike path. That way you could go back and forth really easily. There's not that much to see on the Brooklyn side."

"You can take my bike, Zoe!" added Debbie. "It's got a good lock and rides well."

Zoe looked at Basti. She could tell he liked the idea.

"But what are we going to tell mom?" asked Debbie. "I'm not sure she's going to like the idea that we let them go by themselves."

"We'll tell her that we wanted to go by bike and there weren't enough bikes for the four of us," said Basti.

"Yeah, it will be fun to be on our own, for once."

Zoe got her camera ready while Basti checked their route. They were about to ride off when Rick grabbed Basti's arm.

"Wait a second," said Rick. "Watch out for yellow cabs! The only thing important to them is picking up their next customer. They sometimes even go through red lights. Also, New Yorkers like to use their horns. It's just the way they communicate – they're like little kids, beeping and honking their horns just to let you know they are there – Honk! Honk!"

☆

"Oh, and one more thing, guys," said Rick stepping back from the bicycle to look at his cousins and his sister. "If mom and dad ask about what I did today, I'm going to tell them that I played frisbee in the park with my friends and then came back here. OK? I'm not going to tell them about the street stickers. They don't think I should be doing that stuff – you know, violating public space, etcetera. So, please, don't say anything to them about it. All right?"

"Sure, sure," said Basti and Zoe. Debbie was silent. The sun was in her eyes and she was squinting as she looked at her brother.

"OK, we're off!" said Basti.

"Have a great time! See you later!" called Debbie and Rick as Basti and Zoe rode away in the direction of Ground Zero. The Meyers lived on the west side of Manhattan Island, so

Basti and Zoe biked to the east side to reach the bridge that crosses the East River into Brooklyn.

There it was: across from the old City Hall – it looked like a huge gate leading onto the river. The bridge itself was held up by thick cables that soared up into the sky. After a few minutes they were on the path that ran along the middle of the bridge. Cars drove in three lanes below the footpath on both sides. Basti and Zoe were riding east, into the sun which had just come up over the stone, brick and concrete buildings of Brooklyn.

"Hey, Basti! Stop! Basti! It's just a quick shot, Basti! Please!" called Zoe from a few meters back. She wanted to get a picture of the blue painted Manhattan Bridge which also crossed over to Brooklyn upriver. She also just had to take a few shots of the people walking on the bridge: the man in dreadlocks dancing down the footpath on in-line skates, and the two white-haired old men walking slowly side-by-side, their hands held behind their backs as if they were having some important philosophical talk.

"Come on, Zoe, I'm tired of waiting!" said Basti in an exasperated voice. "Let's go!"

After a short rest at a park on the Brooklyn side they got back on their bikes for the trip back. The view of downtown Manhattan this way was much more dramatic: the mirrored facades of the closely built office buildings in the background and the lower buildings along the water in front of them. Zoe was in the middle of a panoramic series looking right down the walking path when something caught her eye. She put down her camera and squinted in the bright light. Walking directly towards Zoe and Basti was a heavy-set teenager wearing a blue T-shirt, khaki shorts and high-top red sneakers. She had seen the boy before. She looked up at the boy's face. No question – it was him, Moog! He came closer with a bouncy step, smiling. "Hey, bro! It's Basti, right? The frankfurter – Rick's cousin! How's it going, man?" Moog held up his hand and the two did a confused version of a soul shake.

"We're good, really good," said Basti.

"Where's Rick?" said Moog looking beyond them. "That's his bicycle, right? I haven't seen the main dude since we were painting up the walls in the Freedom Tunnel. What's he up to?"

"That's strange – he said he was going to meet up with you today," said Basti thoughtfully.

"Not me, man. I haven't even spoken to him on the phone. Maybe you mean Raul. He's the tall skinny guy."

"Yeah, of course I remember," said Basti, a bit irritated by this strange meeting.

"Well, Raul said something about checking out another tunnel. I don't know exactly – maybe an old subway tunnel. I've been out of touch for a few days, working on my music. I play the drums. Anyway, where are you guys going?" said Moog, starting to rock back and forth on the soles of his sneakers.

"We're going to the Lower East Side," said Basti.

"Oh, yeah? What are you doing there?"

"Oh, we're just going to look around," said Basti, not wanting to talk about Mr. Kaminski. "And then we're going to meet Rick and his family in Chinatown."

"Yeah, that's cool. Well, I don't want to interrupt your ride. Say hello to Rick for me. Tell him that his friend Moog is on the move. I'm sure he's not going to believe that we bumped into each other just like that. Pretty cool. I've got to go, but have a good one, my man!" said Moog, sending a nod also in Zoe's direction before starting to walk on.

"That was really strange," said Basti shaking his head.

☆

"There it is! One thirty-one Orchard Street!" said Basti pointing to a five-story brick building. "That's the fire escape. He used to sit there ..." Zoe looked up and saw a woman who was sitting on an orange blanket on the third level of the fire escape. She was reading a newspaper and slowly drinking from a coffee cup.

But *Kaminski's Hats* was gone. It had been replaced with two stores: *International Luggage* and *M.S.Fashions*. The two little shops were squeezed into the ground floor space.

Outside *International Luggage – Trunks & Travel Bags*, suitcases of all shapes and colors lined the sidewalk. Basti and Zoe parked and locked up their bikes and entered the store. Inside, its walls were covered from floor to ceiling

with bags and suitcases of every size. The little store felt dark and cramped. An Asian woman was standing at the back of the store, unpacking small black leather backpacks and hanging them with a clothes pin on a long wire that spanned the length of the tiny store.

"Hello," she said softly, "can I help you?"

"We're just looking," said Basti, picking up a red and black nylon sport bag from the floor and throwing the strap over his shoulder.

"How much is this?" he asked.

"Nineteen ninety-nine," answered the woman.

"Hmm," said Basti and put it back carefully on the floor. He liked the bag, but he was really interested in seeing if any of the original shelves from *Kaminski's Hats* might be hiding behind all these bags.

"Thanks," they said, walking out the door. Out on the street, Zoe took several pictures of the building. She made sure she got one which showed the facade as a whole. Orchard Street still felt like it was part of an old neighborhood. It was narrow and few of the buildings had more than five stories. Many of the shops on the street sold leather goods and luggage. And although the names and owners of the shops had changed, the street was still lined with stores as Mr. Kaminski had said. The people had changed too. The Bernsteins, Fischls, Rosenbergs and Goldmans were gone. The shops were now owned by Chinese-Americans, Lebanese-Americans and Hispanics. Directly across the street from *International Luggage* was a store called *World Hats*. You could see the traces of the past in the large brick building across the street from Mr. Kaminski's childhood home. Painted on the facade were the words: *S. Beckenstein • World's Largest Selection Woolens Silks and Best Value*. At the ground level was a store called *World Hats*. Drawn by the signs, Basti and Zoe crossed over to *World Hats* and went right in. It was great. Hats galore. Basti tried on Stetsons, straw Pork Pie hats, simple black hats, newspaper boy caps and even a shiny top hat. Zoe took photos of Basti as he posed with each one.

"What are you looking for?" asked the shopkeeper, clearly not pleased with the two teenagers. "They try on everything in the shop, have fun and then they don't buy anything and just leave," thought the woman.

"I don't know," said Basti.

"OK, no more photos. You buy first and then you can take photos. OK?" The man handed him a black hat and smiled. "This one is better for you. Try." It had a smaller rim than the others and a black silk band. It fit well and felt good. Basti pulled it into his face like a gangster and looked in the mirror. He liked what he saw.

"How much?" he asked the shopkeeper.

"Thirty dollars. That one is from Italy. Very fine hat, that one. It looks good." Basti took another look in the mirror. Then he took it off, looked inside and put it back on. It felt as if it belonged on his head.

"Was meinst du, Zoe?"

"Sieht toll aus, aber ganz schön teuer, oder?" she answered. But a few seconds later, Zoe made a thumbs up sign and nodded her head. The shopkeeper smiled and Basti walked out of *World Hats* wearing an Italian felt hat.

☆

Basti and Zoe pushed open the door to *Wong Fat*. They were met by a smiling Chinese man who rather loudly asked "Table for two?" as he brought them into the dining area. Next to the entrance was a small area bordered on one side by hanging, toffee-colored smoked ducks, a steel stick threaded through their necks.

Zoe hopped in reflex when she heard a sharp chop, chop. The man behind the duck curtain was cutting a duck into

small pieces. In seconds the pieces were slipped into a plastic container, which in turn was slid into a brown paper bag and given over to a waiting customer.

"No, no," explained Basti, we are meeting our uncle here, Mr. Meyer."

"Oh! You with Mr. Meyer! I see ... Good, good. Come with me." The man brought them deeper into the dining room where waiters were racing past, carrying several dishes at once on large metal trays. Turning his head around to speak with them as he continued to walk forward, the man said, "Yeah, Mr. Meyer not here yet. He called and said he come very soon. OK?" Basti and Zoe nodded.

"Here is Mr. Meyer's table. Please. Sit." The man sat them at a large round table. Soon after six menus were brought to the table, six little tea cups and a pot of hot tea. Just then Aunt Marion and Uncle Ben appeared at the door followed by Debbie. The small man met them at the door and in that loud voice said, "Welcome, Mr. Meyer, yeah, your friends are already here."

"Sorry we're late! It was really impossible to find a parking space. I'm so happy that you were able to find the restaurant. Come on, Ben, why don't you sit over there and Debbie, you sit next to Zoe," she said excitedly. "Excuse me, I must use the ladies' room. Darling – you can go ahead and order. I'll be right back."

Marion rushed off to the bathroom. Uncle Ben sat back and laughed. "You would think that we were two hours late! It's only ten past six. Have you been waiting long?"

"No," said Basti, "we got here just five minutes ago."

"Well, Marion hates to be even one minute late! Well, never mind ... I hope you are all hungry. This restaurant is one of the best in Chinatown. You wouldn't think so from the décor, but the food is very authentic. You see, look around. It's full of Chinese. That means it's good." Uncle Ben poured himself a cup of tea and opened the menu.

"Who likes salt and peppered deep-fried squid? *Das ist frittierter Tintenfisch*. Or pork dumpling – *Schweineknödel*? How about smoked duck?" To Basti and Zoe, Uncle Ben could have been speaking Chinese. They had never heard of any of these things. The only Chinese dishes they had eaten were mini spring rolls, chicken fried noodles and beef with broccoli.

"Well listen, I'm going to order, and I want you to try everything. If you don't like something, that's fine, you just have to give it a fair chance. OK?" Zoe and Basti nodded, hoping that Uncle Ben would also order something 'normal'. They were both pretty hungry from riding around all day.

"Have you ordered yet?" said Aunt Marion as she returned to the table.

"No, I wanted to wait for you. And Rick isn't here yet."

"But where is he? I thought he was with you two," said Aunt Marion, looking at Basti and Zoe.

"Rick said he was going to the park to play frisbee with some friends," answered Basti.

"And why didn't he go with you?"

"Well, we wanted to go across the Brooklyn Bridge today. There were only two bikes, so Zoe and I went alone."

"Really? That's too bad," said Aunt Marion, looking surprised and slightly annoyed.

"Well, I guess if you two can find this place on your own, you don't need any guide," said Uncle Ben. "Let's order and then I want to hear all about your day ..."

"Oh! Look!" Aunt Marion pointed to the door. "Here comes Rick now."

Rick looked tired. He walked over to their table, and slumped down in the empty chair between Debbie and Aunt Marion. His mother filled his tea cup.

"Drink up, dear, that will make you feel better," she said softly. As Rick picked up his cup, Basti saw a spot of black paint on his middle finger and one on his thumbs.

"You must have played a hard game of frisbee – I hope you won the game," said Uncle Ben.

"Well, we didn't actually play a game. We were just throwing the disc around. But we did a lot of running around. A lot of sun and a lot of people, that's all."

Aunt Marion took a good look at Rick. "You don't look well. I'm a little worried. For all that playing in the sun, you look very pale. You look like a ghost. Are you really feeling all right?"

"Yes, Mom, I'm fine. Really! Don't worry about it. I'm just a bit tired, that's all."

The dishes arrived at the table.

"I'm sure you'll like this – go on, try one," said Uncle Ben pushing one of the plates towards Basti. Three shining white crepes rolled with shrimp were laid waiting on the white dish. Basti slid one of the fat noodle-like things onto his plate and tried to pick it up with his chopsticks. It slipped right back on the plate. After a few more tries, Basti gave up and picked it up with his knife and fork, dipped it in a dark sauce and ate. It was delicious! Soon after, a plate of smoked duck arrived on the table. Oh, and this, Basti thought, must be the *Tintenfisch* – whatever that was in English. It was squid – crunchy, spicy and good. Next came a plate of fried noodles, a beef dish, a whole fish, a chicken dish and six bowls of delicious rice. It was a great dinner. Rick didn't say much while Zoe and Basti spoke about their bike trip across the bridge, and their walk through the Lower East Side.

"Oh yeah, Rick, we also met your friend Moog," said Zoe. "He was walking across the Brooklyn Bridge. He told us to tell you that 'Moog is on the move!'"

"What's that supposed to mean?" asked Uncle Ben, "*Moog is on the move.* That friend of yours has the strangest name I've ever heard. What's his real name? I'm sure his parents didn't write Moog on his birth papers!"

"It's Jeff, Dad. His real name is Jeff Knowles."

"I can't believe you met Moog on the Brooklyn Bridge!" said Debbie turning to Rick for an answer.

Rick kept silent, lifting another bite of noodles into his mouth.

☆

When they came home from the restaurant, Rick went right to bed while the others watched 'Live and Let Die', an old James Bond film, on television.

It was about eight o'clock in the morning when Basti was woken by the sound of the front door closing as Uncle Ben and Aunt Marion left for work.

"Basti, are you awake?"

"Yeah, what's up?" answered Basti.

"Well, I'd like to explain about yesterday. It was a bit complicated and I didn't like how things turned out."

"OK, go on, I'm listening."

"You know, the Freedom Tunnel isn't the only place which has not been used for a while. There are other tunnels and ghost stations."

"Ghost stations?" asked Basti lifting his head up from the bed to see if Rick was just joking around.

But Rick's face was still pale and he wasn't smiling.

"Yeah, yesterday Raul and I went down to a ghost station on 91st Street. It's part of the old IRT line. In the 1950s the subway system was rebuilt. New stations and new trains were added. The whole system got much bigger and the new trains are longer – five cars instead of three. The problem was that the new trains are too long for the old stations. It cost too much to rebuild all the old stations, so some were just closed – they became ghost stations. Trains just didn't stop there any more. There are about four in the city. And yesterday I was in the 91st Street ghost station, which is way uptown on the east side. I went with Raul, just Raul. It's not the kind of place you want to go with too many people. That's why I didn't tell you, Basti. I just couldn't ask everybody, and especially not Debbie. I think she is going to tell mom and dad all about the Freedom Tunnel. And I just didn't want to get you into trouble, you know? Mom and dad don't even like the fact that I put up street stickers. I really wanted to take you along yesterday, because it's a really cool place. But I had the feeling that if I told you about it, you would say you want to ask Zoe. And then Zoe would talk about it to Debbie and the whole thing would get out of control. I'm really sorry about lying to you. I'm sure you felt pretty strange when you met Moog yesterday after I said that I was going over to his house. That sucks, man!"

"Yeah, it wasn't so cool, and I didn't feel good about lying to your mom and dad. But I understand a little better now."

"Sorry, man."

"So did you make some new graffiti?"

"Yeah, I did – and I think it's my best so far. I added another color. This one's not just black and white. The Borg is yellow and has a purple shadow. I worked on it for four hours. Many trains went by. But I didn't even really hear them – I was concentrating so hard. Raul was with me, but he was working about 20 feet away. I had just finished my Borg, I stood back to look at it and saw Raul running towards me. He was running fast, and I knew what that meant. He had seen a policeman checking the station and any moment he would find us. I picked up my spray cans, threw them into my bag and ran. Not only did we have to move quickly, we had to run as quietly as possible. That was the hard part. Although 91st Street was a real station, the entry stair is gone. You have to run along the tracks to 96th Street and then jump back up to the platform. It's really not that far because the end of the 96th Street Station is at 94th Street. But still, man, my heart was beating so hard I thought it would jump out of my body!"

"But you made it, right?" asked Basti.

"Yeah, of course we made it, or I wouldn't be here to tell you this story. But it was a really close call ... and dangerous – really dangerous. If a train had come when we were running to the other station we could have been hurt. And there was also the chance that somebody who saw us climbing up at the end of the station could report us to the police. Oh man, it was too much!"

Chapter 8

Rick didn't actually get out of bed that day. After speaking with Basti, he just dropped his head back onto his pillow.

"I'm just going to stay in bed a little longer, Basti. I'll be up soon." Basti left the room quietly, had breakfast and took a shower. When he came back to get dressed he found Rick still fast asleep. By 12 o'clock Debbie thought they'd better wake him up.

"This is really strange," she said, "he never sleeps this late. He might be sick." She entered the room and spoke softly to her brother. She felt his forehead like she had seen her mother do many times.

"He's still out – but his temperature is OK," said Debbie entering the living room.

"I guess he got too much sun yesterday playing frisbee," said Zoe smiling.

"Yeah, right," said Debbie.

"Are we going to stay in all day?" asked Zoe, flipping through a magazine she had found on the living room table. "I'd like to do something."

"And leave Rick alone?" said Basti.

"Well, he's not sick," said Debbie. "Maybe he has another secret plan, and he's just waiting for us to leave before he sneaks out."

"I know!" said Zoe suddenly throwing down the magazine and jumping up from the couch. "Let's go and take a ride on the Statue of Liberty Ferry boat. You and Rick both said it was a great ride."

"That's not a bad idea," said Debbie. "I'm up for that. Basti, why don't you go and talk to Rick. Maybe you can convince him to get out of bed and come with us. I don't think he wants to talk to me."

"OK, I'll try."

When he entered the bedroom this time, even Basti noticed the old pajama smell. The room was still dark except for the glow of Rick's computer. Rick was sitting in front of the screen, hitting the arrow buttons on his keyboard.

"Hey Rick, how is it going?"

"I'm in the fifth level of this game. I've never done that before … Oh no!" The GAME OVER message appeared on the screen and Rick turned to Basti.

"What's up?" he asked.

"We're going to go for a ride on the Statue of Liberty Ferry boat and then we'll maybe pick up some lunch on the way back. Are you interested?" asked Basti.

"Sorry, bro," said Rick shaking his head. "I'm staying in today. I don't feel like going anywhere." He turned back to the screen and began hitting the keys on his keyboard again. Basti picked up his backpack and started walking towards the door.

"See you later," said Basti quietly.

"Yeah," said Rick without even turning to look at Basti.

☆

"Hey, we could also take the Staten Island Ferry," said Debbie as they rode down in the elevator. "It takes a bit longer but it's free. We don't have to pay a cent to get on." Zoe was holding her camera up to her eye and tried to photograph Debbie's hand in the mirror.

"How long is the ride?" asked Basti.

"I think it's about twenty minutes or half an hour. I'm not really sure. To be honest, I don't even remember what Staten Island is like, even though we spent half a year there after

9/11." They reached the ground floor and marched outside.

☆

The ferry backed away from the tip end of lower Manhattan. With a group of other passengers, tourists like themselves, they stood on the boat's lower rear deck, watching and waving goodbye to Manhattan – its skyline squeezing together and becoming smaller and smaller until it looked like it could fit into one of those plastic bubbles that you can shake and make the snow flakes inside float, flutter and fall. From out here, Manhattan seemed to float on the water.

☆

On the way back home, they stopped at the local photo shop and picked up prints of Zoe's last photos.

Later, sitting on the balcony, they passed the new prints round. There were photos of their day in Coney Island, the Brooklyn Bridge, Orchard Street and even of the Chinese Restaurant. Then came the photos of the Freedom Tunnel: the pictures of Zoe, Basti and Rick's first visit and then the second time. Zoe had the picture of Basti and Mr. Kaminski in her hand. She looked up at Basti and Debbie. It was as if they all had the same idea at the same moment.

"Should we go now or tomorrow?" asked Zoe.

"Tomorrow," said Basti and Debbie together.

"It might already be too dark if we went now," he said.

☆

It was 12:15 on the next day when they reached the tunnel's entrance. After the 12:25 train passed, they ran almost the whole way to Mr. Kaminski's office. There was a crack of light under his door. They knocked and heard his voice say "*Herein*!"

"That's what he said last time I was here," whispered Basti in Debbie's ear.

"Welcome, very happy to see you. But I'm sorry to say, young ladies, that I'm afraid I will disappoint you today. My sister Shari is in Florida now. She's taking care of her two grandchildren while their parents take a little vacation. In other words I don't have the hats I promised you."

"That's OK, Mr. Kaminski, we didn't come here for the hats, we came to show you some photos that Zoe took," said Debbie warmly.

Zoe gave him the pictures. He went through them one by one. At each photo, he smiled, nodded his head and said, "Fine, fine!" Some of them he held up and said, "Now that's a good one!"

When he got to the photo of Orchard Street he looked at the picture for a long time and finally said, "That's my home! 131 Orchard Street. I lived there! I know those windows! You took a photo of the fire escape! There's a woman sitting exactly where I used to sit. My God, after all these years ..." Mr. Kaminski looked at the next photo. "and that's *S. Beckenstein's* – right across the street! Yes! *World's Largest Selection Woolens Silks*. I remember standing on the fire escape and trying to look at the people who worked at *Beckenstein's*. This brings back a lot! How marvelous! *Wunderbar*! Thank you. What a surprise. But, tell me, what's the street like now? What else did you see?"

"There are a lot of shops," said Basti.

"Full of things," added Zoe, "suitcases, bags and hats."

"Hats?" asked Mr. Kaminski looking up.

"And lots of leather shops," added Basti.

"Yeah, hats. You see this place?" said Zoe. "That's where Basti bought his hat. He tried so many on! Then the man gave him this one and he bought it!"

"Let me see," said Mr. Kaminski. Basti passed him the hat. Mr. Kaminski looked inside, squeezed the outside and drew his finger around its rim.

"How much did you pay for this?" he asked.

"Thirty dollars."

"Not bad, not bad. All I can say is, don't wear it in the rain, or you won't have a hat any more, you'll have a black shopping bag. You know what I mean, my boy?"

Mr. Kaminski gave Basti back the hat. "So let's see where else my friends have been," he said and turned back to the rest of the photos.

"Ah, the Brooklyn Bridge. A monument to man's genius and passion." He stared at the photos of the Brooklyn Bridge as if looking for something.

"You know, there is a story behind the building of the Brooklyn Bridge," said Mr. Kaminski. "It's the story of the Roebling family. First there was the great John Roebling, the father. He was a German immigrant, you know, who came to America when he was 25. He was a very successful bridge engineer. He had designed and built a number of beautiful bridges before he got it in his head to build a bridge over the East River and link Manhattan and Brooklyn. To really understand what a distance that is, you need to see the Brooklyn Bridge from the side. It just goes on and on and the long deck is hung from these cables. Herr Roebling made these strong cables by twisting thinner wires together into strong metal rope. It was to be the longest suspension bridge in the world. Well, the building of the bridge began, and like they do on all big projects, Roebling took some important men on a tour of the site. It was just the first week and – Bang! A big piece of wood fell on Mr. Roebling's foot, crushing it completely. The doctors had to cut it off. You can live without a foot, of course, but the wound became infected and he died soon after. Well, his son, Washington Roebling, then took over the work of directing the bridge's construction. But he was almost as unlucky as his father. You see, the bridge is hung from two great towers that were built in the river. To build the towers' foundations, they had to dig under the river's water. It was horrible work – some people have said it was like being in hell! What is 'hell' in German?"

"*Die Hölle,*" said Basti.

"Yes, of course ... die Hölle. Well, they worked in a large wood box that was lowered down to the bottom of the river. It's just like when you push an empty, upside down glass straight down in a sink full of water. The glass never fills with water. That's how they worked – in this large wood box with no bottom. Well, Washington was down there every day with all the rest of the workers making sure the work went well. But, in that same year he got 'caisson's disease'. It's what deep sea divers get when they come up from the bottom of the sea too quickly. I'm no doctor – hah! – but what I understand is that a bubble of oxygen forms in the blood and it makes you very sick. Washington spent the rest of his life in a wheelchair, in fact he almost died. But the Roebling family didn't give up. Washington taught his wife, Emily, all about the maths behind the bridge's design and about the materials that were used for its construction. For the next eleven years, it was his wife, Emily Roebling, who watched over the work on the bridge. In that time, let me tell you, it wasn't easy for a woman to do a man's work, but she was a very intelligent woman and she kept on fighting! She was also the first person to walk across the bridge in 1883, something her husband was never able to do because of his illness. In fact, he never visited the construction site but watched the building through a telescope from his apartment window.

There's one more part of the story. One week after the bridge opened, many people paid 5 cents for the chance to walk across. The bridge was full with people. Somebody on the bridge started screaming that the bridge was going to fall. Well, in those days, there were still a lot of people who believed no bridge could be so long and so strong. People got nervous and started running trying to get off as fast as they could. They pushed and shoved and panic broke out. Twelve people were run over and killed in the rush. To show people that the bridge was really safe, P.T. Barnum of New York's biggest circus, Barnum & Bailey's Circus, had his famous elephant Jumbo lead twenty elephants across the bridge.

What they did with the elephants on the other side? Ha! I'll never know! The Brooklyn Bridge took 13 years to build and 27 men died during construction including the great Roebling himself. To me, next to the old Penn Station the Brooklyn Bridge is one of the most beautiful structures in New York. Quite a story, eh?" Mr. Kaminski took one last look at the photograph he still held in his hand and then gave them back to Zoe.

"I've got something for you," he said. Mr. Kaminski got slowly up from his chair, looked through the many rolls of paper and pulled out a tall roll from an open box of maps.

"Here ... just wait a moment – there is a special one I am looking for." He brought one to the table, unrolled it and shook his head. It was an architectural drawing. "No, that's not right. That's the plan." Debbie, Basti and Zoe stayed in their chairs following the old man's every movement. They had no idea what to expect. Mr. Kaminski pulled out another roll, brought it to the table and unrolled it.

"Aah! This is it!" he said flattening out the picture with his hand. His hand went over the fine lines of a panoramic view of the Brooklyn Bridge. It was an old brown line print, with traces of other colors.

"This is for both of you. I want you to take it back to Germany. It's Roebling's bridge. And look, Zoe, here in the corner is a portrait of Emily Roebling, the woman who brought the work to completion, the woman who linked one side of New York to the other."

Zoe was impressed. It was a beautiful picture and an unusual souvenir of New York. Mr. Kaminski rolled up the picture and handed it to Basti.

"And it's your job to bring it back safely to German ground, hah!"

It was time to leave. Debbie and Zoe moved towards the door. Basti lingered behind. Mr. Kaminski leaned in close to Basti's ear. "How did the relic search go, my boy?" As if expecting Mr. Kaminski to ask, but still not prepared, Basti managed to say, "I haven't gone yet, but ..."

"I know you'll go. Take your time, you'll go. But I want to see the pictures of what you've found. I know those things exist. I've seen them with my own eyes. I'd still like to know what's changed."

Basti could feel Mr. Kaminski's passion for the relics becoming his own.

"I'll come back and show you," said Basti, not quite sure of what it was he was promising to do.

"*Auf Wiedersehen*!" said Mr. Kaminski, standing on the little landing in front of his office door.

"*Auf Wiedersehen,*" answered first Zoe and then Basti, waving as they backed away.

Debbie also waved and said "bye-bye" in a sweet and childish way.

While walking back to the entrance of the tunnel Basti put his black hat back on his head, tilting it slightly to the left. He did a little quick step dance in and out of the clear rays of white light.

Chapter 9

Ever since his trip to the ghost station, Rick had been acting strange. He didn't go outdoors and stayed at home for the next three days surfing on the Internet watching short clips of skateboarders, DJs and graffiti artists on YouTube or sitting on the balcony just watching people go by.

Uncle Ben and Aunt Marion had taken a few days off work to spend time with Zoe and Basti during their last week in New York. It was Sunday and the whole family had been invited to friends for brunch. The plan was to go to the brunch and then to Central Park for an open-air jazz concert. Zoe and Debbie had gone with Uncle Ben and Aunt Marion. But Rick just said there was no way he was going to spend his Sunday afternoon sitting around with boring adults, eating smelly French cheese with 'baguette' and drinking champagne and orange juice. Basti decided to stay behind too, thinking he and Rick could do something together.

Basti was in the living room looking at the print of the Brooklyn Bridge that Mr. Kaminski had given him when he heard Rick's voice calling him.

"Hey Basti, you've got to come and see this." Basti found Rick in his usual position in front of his computer screen. This time he was looking at photos of graffiti.

"Here is some of Freedom's early work. He was one of the first to paint on subway trains. He did it in a train yard outside the city. And look, that's him," said Rick clicking on a picture of a young guy with light brown hair.

"Doesn't he look like a regular guy? In an interview he said that it took him a while to get accepted in a graffiti gang. They were all tough street kids. But later on he really became the leader and the most famous of his group just because his work was so awesome." Rick seemd to know everything about this young man.

"We saw his work in the Freedom Tunnel, right?"

"Yup, some of his best work is down there."

"You know, Rick, speaking of the Freedom Tunnel, I was thinking about going to Penn Station to look for those old things Mr. Kaminski wrote down. Maybe we could both go there today – what do you think?" said Basti in a soft voice. He unfolded the list of locations Mr. Kaminski had written down for him.

"Why would you want to do that? What did he call them – relics? An old stone eagle and an old staircase? I mean, come on, bro! Those don't exactly sound like thrilling discoveries!"

"Yeah, but he asked me to come back and tell him what I found. And he gave me these beautiful old photos and the Brooklyn Bridge print."

"Man, Basti, Kaminski is a bit of a nut – you know, crazy," said Rick, typing in another website address. "He probably found those old prints and maps in the garbage bin of the New York Public Library. That old guy spends the whole day underground in a dark tunnel. I mean, you never know, maybe he's making it all up about working for the train company as a 'track man'. And anyway, you don't ever have to see him again. Here, let me see that paper." Rick grabbed the soft piece of paper out of Basti's hand, tearing off one corner. On it Mr. Kaminski had listed all the 'relics' and their exact locations so that Basti could find them in Penn Station.

"Yeah, just what I thought," continued Rick, pointing at the letterhead. "Look at this: it says 'U.S. Army Veterans'

Hospital, Meadow Park, N.Y.'. Kaminski has probably been living in a mental institution – you know, a place for crazy people – for people with a few screws loose."

Basti didn't like the way Rick was talking. No, not one bit. He had a tight feeling in his chest and it felt as if something was stuck in the back of his throat. He really didn't like the way Rick was talking – it was ugly and mean.

"I'm going out," said Basti without looking at his cousin.

"Hey, I'm sorry, I didn't mean to hurt your feelings. I'm just telling you the way I see it, and I am a New Yorker. You know I live here. I can read people better than you can. I've got the background. But go and check it out if you want. I'm not going to stop you. I can ..."

But Basti didn't want to hear what Rick could do or what he was going to say. He picked up his bag and was out the door, down the elevator and out in the street. Walking, walking ... He reached the Battery Park promenade, which over the last week had become a familiar background.

"I'm going," he said quietly to himself. "And I'm going NOW."

From that point on, everything went like clockwork. Down the steps to the number 1 uptown local subway, metro-card in slot, train pulled into the station. Basti stayed standing, tall and thin, watching people as the train filled up. He passed Canal and Christopher Street, 14th, and 23rd Street. When the train pulled into 34th Street Basti got out and followed the signs for Penn Station. At the top of the stairs he pulled out the paper and the photo from Mr. Kaminski from his back pocket.

First the eagle, he thought as he got to the corner of 33rd Street and 7th Avenue. OK, down to 31st and look out for a

fallen stone eagle! Looking for a big stone bird meant looking at and then beyond everything else – the fifty-floor tower at Penn Plaza, an oversized yellow and blue umbrella where a dark-haired man was selling hot dogs from a metal wagon. Most of all, he looked through the hundreds of people walking quickly past him. And then there it was: on a five-foot high block with a metal fence around it and a few typical city bushes – the eagle. He wanted to climb over the fence to get a close-up view and wished he had planned the trip a bit better. He wished he could take a photo of the eagle to show Mr. Kaminski that he had found it. He took out the photo of the old station and tried to imagine where this eagle might have been fifty years ago. When he opened his bag he saw his sketchbook. He had planned to make sketches of New York, but had never actually done it. This time he took out the sketchbook and a pencil and did a quick drawing. Not yet happy with it, he made a second one, this time adding more of the context. In the bottom corner he wrote Penn Station Eagle, NYC and the date. He put the sketchbook quickly back in his bag. He felt strangely embarrassed to be drawing a picture of old things in this modern, fast moving city.

Behind the eagle was one of the main entrances to the train station. He moved slowly as if he wanted to remember something, as if he were an actor in a movie. As he got closer to the entrance it was like stepping into a fast moving river – only instead of water, this river was made of moving people going down the escalators and the stairs on their way back home. Rush hour.

Basti found the staircase easily. It was the only one with a shiny metal ball at the top railing. He stood at the top of the stairs. He walked down to the bottom. He looked at the digitized sign box which showed the time and destination of the next few trains. He slowly walked back up the steps. Although it was an old staircase he didn't feel anything special about it. In fact, like Rick had said, it wasn't an exciting discovery – it was just an old staircase. Standing at the top he felt the up and down push and pull of people hurrying to their trains or to a meeting somewhere in the city. He, Basti, wasn't going anywhere. Still unsure of what to draw, he pulled out his sketchbook. There were so many hands reaching for the shiny brass ball at the top of the stairs. That's what he would draw: the ball and a hand. People were pushing him. Some looked at what he was drawing. He felt in the way. He went down to the bottom of the steps and made another sketch of the many bodies coming down the stairs. When many came down together, it looked like one mass with many heads.

"5:14 for Newark, Trenton, Princeton and Philadelphia. All Aaaaboard!"

Basti listened to the scratchy sound of the announcements over the loudspeakers. The announcement was repeated and this time Basti recorded it on his cellphone. It was time to move on. Basti took out Mr. Kaminski's list again. He looked down at the next item and read '3. Track indicator; location: baggage area next to Track 1'.

What is a track indicator? he thought to himself. He had to know what he was looking for before wandering around this big station. Track – *das ist doch auf Deutsch das Gleis, und* indicator *ist ein Indikator – oder*? Still, the German word *Gleisindikator* brought no image to his mind. Basti looked back at the paper. He had missed the little sketch Mr. Kaminski had made next to the description. There was an arrow from the word 'Track indicator' to a drawing, but the drawing wasn't on the little piece of paper. Basti read on: 'Look for the object marked by a red circle in photo #2 of the old Penn Station.' But this didn't help much either. He had left all the other photos at home.

Basti looked up and found the sign for Track 1 and the baggage claim area and headed in that direction. The baggage area was not much more than a light green counter in front of a row of metal shelves where boxes and suitcases were kept. Basti went up to the counter. No one was there.

"Just a moment, I'm coming," said a very large woman in a blue uniform and soft white shoes. She waddled slowly up to the counter breathing quite heavily. Then she plopped down in a folding chair behind the counter.

"Can I help you you?" she asked after taking a few more noisy breaths.

"Yes, I ..."

"I need to see your ticket, honey," she said before Basti could even finish his sentence.

"Uh, I'm not actually picking up anything, today," said Basti, "I'm looking for a track indicator."

"A what?" she asked turning her head up as if to say that she hadn't heard correctly.

"An old track indicator," repeated Basti.

"I never heard of an 'old track indicator'. The information desk is in the main hall. You'd better go ask there. There's no such thing here, you can be sure of that."

"I'm sorry, I mean I'm looking for a relic," said Basti, still convinced that what he was looking for was somewhere behind the green counter.

"A what?"

"A relic!"

The lady shook her head and started making those heavy breathing sounds again.

"I've never heard of a track indicator or a relic! Like I said, the information desk in in the main hall. This is baggage claim here. All we've got is baggage. That's all, just bags and boxes, see?"

Still Basti was not ready to give up. "I'm probably not saying it well. I'm German and my English is not so good. I'm looking for something that was part of the Old Penn Station. Maybe if you let me come behind the counter, I could look for it myself."

"Listen, honey, the only person that is going to look for something behind this counter is me. If you don't have a baggage claim ticket, I can't help you." The lady sat there, breathing heavily and started tapping her fat finger tips on the counter. Basti looked at her big face but still didn't feel ready to turn away. He had an idea. He would show the lady Mr. Kaminski's photo of the old Penn Station.

"I'm going to show you something, and then maybe you'll understand me better," said Basti and lifted his backpack onto the counter.

"Excuse me," she said in an angry tone, "I think you'd better go now or I'm going to have to call security." Basti started to unzip his backpack.

"Just a moment, please," he said, sticking his hand inside the bag to get the photo out.

"Like I said, you'd better go to the information desk right now or I'm going to have to call security." Maybe the lady had pressed a button under the counter because just then a security guard in uniform appeared swinging a dark brown wood stick.

"Is everything all right here?" he asked.

"Officer," said the fat lady, "I asked this young man for a baggage claim ticket. First he says he doesn't have one. Then he says he is looking for something he thinks is in the baggage claim area. I told him several times that he should go to the information desk if he has a special question. And then, he starts fishing in his bag for something and …"

"Right. I'll take care of it from here. Can you please follow me?" said the guard. He led Basti through a door, down a small corridor and then through another door to a small office room with a noisy air-conditioner.

"I'm going to have to check your bag."

"Check my bag?" asked Basti surprised.

"It's just for security, son."

"Sure," said Basti handing his blue backpack over to the man. He watched as the officer took out his wallet, his pens and pencils, a baseball cap and a half pack of chewing gum.

As he took out the sketchbook the old photo slipped out and landed on the floor. The officer picked it up, looked at both sides and said nothing. He lifted up the now empty bag and shook it upside down a few times. Quite a bit of Coney Island sand landed on the table. The officer then flipped through Basti's sketchbook.

"Drawings," he said, "what are you doing these drawings for?" he asked.

Why am I doing these drawings? Basti repeated the officer's question in his head. An image of Mr. Kaminski in his office came to Basti's mind. These drawings are for him, he thought.

He quickly said, "It's for a school project about old things in New York."

"Can I see some ID?"

"ID?" asked Basti.

"Identification. You know, a driver's license, student ID, passport," explained the man.

"Well, I'm from Germany and I'm staying with my aunt and uncle here in New York. My passport is at home."

"OK, I'd like you to fill this out and then you can go. There's nothing wrong, we just need this information for the records."

The officer pulled out a piece of paper and handed it to Basti. The form asked for his name, address, telephone number and reason for being in Penn Station. Basti filled out the first part, but wasn't sure how he should answer the last question.

Looking for relics of the old Penn Station? No, that didn't sound right. Then he remembered two English words from school, and he wrote down 'Research Project'. That sounded very good.

Basti gave the officer the paper.

"Is this your uncle's address?"

"Yes, sir."

"Can you please write down your uncle's name and your address in Germany. Basti did as he was told.

"OK, we're finished here then," the man said. "But I don't want to see you asking funny questions again. People here have a job to do. You understand what I mean?"

"Yes, sir."

"OK, then you can go now, and good luck on your research project," he said as he opened the door for Basti.

"Thank you," said Basti. On the door was a small sign. Basti read 'Amtrak Station Security. No Unauthorized Personnel'.

Basti walked out to the main hall. Would the security guard call Uncle Ben? And if he did, what would he say? And what would he, Basti, say when Uncle Ben asked how he ended up in a security guard's office? Well, he would say he was just walking down a street in midtown Manhattan when he saw a stone eagle behind a fence and just started drawing it. He got thirsty and went down into the station to get a drink. And since he was enjoying drawing so much he started drawing everything in sight: staircases, the baggage area and even a security office. It all sounded more or less plausible – a typical activity for a young tourist!

He looked at the fourth item on the list: '4. Two original arches; location: at the end of the IRT subway platform, downtown local'. As Basti had to take that train back to Battery Park City, he decided to go on the search for relic number 4.

It was easy to find. He took out his sketchbook right away and began to draw. It was not long before he had the feeling that somebody was standing behind him, looking over his shoulder. Thinking that the security guard had followed him, Basti spun around. Phew! It was just a regular man – no uniform and no wood stick.

"Didn't mean to scare you," he said. "I was just curious about what you were drawing."

"Yeah, well ..." mumbled Basti. He felt he had done enough explaining already and really just wanted to finish his sketch.

"What are these?" asked the man, pointing to the paper.

"They are old arches," said Basti "they were part of the original Penn Station. I'm doing a research project for school." He starting to believe that this was the safest thing to say. The man could be working undercover.

"Interesting, interesting ... but you're not from here – wait, let me guess, you're from one of those Nordic countries, right? Sweden, Finland or ..."

"No," corrected Basti, "I'm from Germany."

"Right!" said the man, "I knew it was Germany! Munich, Berlin, Stuttgart ... So, tell me, what's your name?"

"Kranbacher, Sebastian Kranbacher."

"Sebastian," he repeated and held out his hand, "good to meet you, my name is Frank Rizzoli. Thanks for the little talk – very interesting ... Oh! There's my train! I got to go – good luck, Sebastian!"

Frank just made it to the train as the doors were closing. Basti saw him turn around and wave through the window. Strange people live in New York, he thought to himself, strange but friendly.

Chapter 10

Basti was riding the 7th Avenue local back home. The train pulled into 23rd Street and he took out Mr. Kaminski's list from his back pocket. He read the heading again: 'U.S. Army Veterans' Hospital, Meadow Park, N.Y.'. Was Mr. Kaminski crazy? Was Rick right? Basti then took out his sketchbook and looked at the day's sketches. He thought he had done a good job of drawing the eagle – not only did it look like an eagle, it looked like a prisoner, but still proud behind the high metal fence. He wasn't as proud of the staircase drawing, but still – he had been there and had drawn what he saw. He turned to the next page which he had reserved for the 'Track Indicator'. Of course he had never been able to draw it. But that is part of the story of my trip, he thought. He had an idea. He began drawing a comic strip of himself – first following the signs for the baggage area, then another of himself speaking to the baggage claim lady. He then drew a series of little sketches of himself being led to the back room by the security guard. Then one of the guard as he emptied his backpack, and of himself writing the words 'Research Project'. In the last sketch he was waving to the officer. Basti made speech bubbles and short captions explaining the action when it was not clear enough from the picture and laughing to himself as he drew. He imagined Mr. Kaminski's surprise when he would see these sketches.

But a shadow passed over Basti's joy when he remembered that he had given the officer Uncle Ben's telephone number. He had thought up an explanation, but what if his uncle started asking Rick and Debbie questions? He had to tell them what had happened and he had to do it fast.

☆

It seemed that Rick hadn't even changed positions. He was still sitting at his computer surfing the Internet.

"Hey Basti, I'm really glad you're back. I'm sorry, man, about what I said. It was really stupid."

"That's OK, but I've got to talk to you. Are Debbie and Zoe here?

"Yeah, I think so. I think they're in Debbie's room."

Basti came back with Debbie and Zoe.

"What's up? Why the big meeting?" asked Debbie as she entered the room. With all of them together, the room felt small and Basti was worried that Uncle Ben or Aunt Marion might walk in on their talk.

"Let's all take a walk down to the promenade," said Basti. "I've got to talk to you all about something."

Debbie and Zoe had been out all day, but they could tell by the seriousness in Basti's voice that this was no time to protest.

As they passed the kitchen on their way out, Aunt Marion called out, "Hey where are you all going? Dinner is in exactly one hour and I don't want to wait! Is that clear?"

"Yes, Mom! We just want to get some fresh air. We'll be back in time. We promise," said Rick.

☆

Basti stood in front of Zoe, Rick and Debbie, who were sitting with open ears on a promenade bench, the Hudson River and the Statue of Liberty in the background.

"I was at Penn Station today," he began, "I was looking for the 'relics' that Mr. Kaminski had told me about and … and … I ran into a little trouble." Basti stopped. He didn't know where to begin, when he remembered the sketchbook and his comic strip. He pulled it out of his bag and handed it to Rick who was sitting between Debbie and Zoe.

"Read this. I think that explains it all." They looked at his sketches and read the comic, sometimes laughing at the images.

"Was this lady really that fat?" asked Zoe.

"She was even bigger in real life," said Basti. "And she was wearing the largest uniform I've ever seen."

"Now wait a second," said Rick. "You said something was wrong – this story is funny! What's the problem, man?" asked Rick looking at Basti.

"Well, I had to give your – I mean Uncle Ben's telephone number to that policeman. And he might just call to check if I am really staying with you. I mean they were asking me questions as if I were a possible terrorist or something!"

"And you're worried that my dad will start asking questions and that he might find out about the Freedom Tunnel. Am I right?" asked Rick.

"Yes, exactly."

"I don't see any problem," said Zoe. "You can just say that you were drawing in and around the station ... and that you found out about the old station and relics on the Internet."

"Yeah, that's true. And we'll all back you up on that story. There is nothing illegal about drawing in a public place like a station. You did absolutely nothing wrong! And your drawings are great!" added Rick.

"They're for Mr. Kaminski. I've got to go one last time but we've only got a few more days left."

"Yeah, tomorrow we're going to a Broadway show with Mom and Dad," said Debbie. "And on Tuesday, I know they want to take you to Harlem, to a baptist church."

"Well, that leaves Wednesday," said Basti. "Who is up for one last trip to the Freedom Tunnel?"

"I am," said Zoe. Rick and Debbie looked down to the ground.

"I've had enough of tunnels for a while," said Rick.

"Yeah, me too, to be honest. It was fun, but I really have a problem with those rats. I don't think I'm ready to come face-to-face with one again," said Debbie, twitching her nose like a rat.

"It looks like you guys will be on your own again," said Rick.

"That's all right, we know the way."

"But I'll tell you what," said Rick, "for all the time you spent down in that dark tunnel, this last time you've got to write something, like 'relic hunter 2009' or I don't know … something!"

Basti stared at Rick. He really had spent a lot of time in that tunnel. But he had no idea what he wanted to write. 'Basti was here' was too childish.

"I'll need to get some spray paint," he said.

"You can use mine!" said Rick excitedly.

"And I don't know how …"

"Look, right after dinner, we'll take a stack of newspaper, my bag of paints, some thick tape and go down to the river beside the piers. We'll be on our own there. I'll show you some tricks and teach you the basics. It'll be easy, I'm sure."

☆

On Tuesday night, Basti carefully put together a booklet of the sketches he had made in Penn Station. There was the picture of the stone eagle, the two sketches of the old staircase and of the arches in the subway station. The drawings were followed by the baggage claim story. Basti titled his comic strip 'The Misadventure of Relic Hunter Basti Kranbacher'. Basti bound all the pages together and added a note on the first page. "Dear Mr. Kaminski," he wrote. "Although I forgot my camera, I made these pictures for you. You'll be glad to know that the proud eagle is still there! Your friend, Sebastian."

Over the weekend, Zoe had made two sets of prints of all the places they had seen in New York. One set was to take home and the other was for Mr. Kaminski. She found an old card game box and put all the photos in there. The top picture was the photo of Basti and Mr. Kaminski that she had made on her second trip. On the top of the box she wrote: "For Mr. Kaminski – Thank you for the beautiful print and your stories! Yours, Zoe Kranbacher, photographer at large." She wasn't actually sure what 'at large' meant. She had seen it once in a book and it just sounded right. "PS," she added at the bottom, "Debbie sends her regards."

☆

They knocked, expecting to hear Mr. Kaminski's voice saying "Herein!" but no one answered. The pushed the door open. It made a creaking sound as it swung open and hit against the inside wall.

"He's not here," said Zoe.

"I can see that," said Basti. Actually as it was very dark in the room, Basti could hardly see anything at all.

"Do you see a light switch?" whispered Zoe, grabbing hold of Basti's arm.

"I'm looking." He felt around the door frame, on one side and then the other.

"Here it is," said Zoe, switching on the light.

They took a deep breath and looked around. Basti felt funny being in the office without Mr. Kaminski. It was a bit like those ghost towns he had seen in so many American Westerns.

Basti took out his booklet from his bag and laid it carefully on the table.

"Do you have your pictures?"

"Yup," said Zoe, and placed the box on top of Basti's book.

☆

Marion folded Zoe's 'I ❤ NY' T-shirt and placed it on top of the stack of clean clothes. She was the only person home. Zoe and Basti had said they would need the morning to buy presents for their parents, Debbie was visiting a friend and Rick and Ben were in the basement garage, trying to install a navigation system. She entered Debbie's room and put the stack of clothes on Zoe's bed. This was their last day. The kids' plane for Frankfurt would leave the next day at 8:25 pm. Seeing that Debbie had left her computer on, she went over to her daughter's desk to turn it off. Next to the computer she noticed a tall stack of photos. On the top was a picture of Debbie in large sunglasses making a funny pose on the river promenade.

"Oh dear!" said Marion to herself. "Those sunglasses are a joke!" She smiled and carefully picked up the photos. She looked at the next. "The Parachute jump, Coney Island," said Marion quietly. There were many pictures of the boardwalk, views of the ocean, and pictures of people lying in the sun. Marion flipped through the rest of the Coney Island pictures quickly. Then she came across a very dark picture. A strong line of sunlight cut across the middle of the image from top to bottom. The photo showed a woman in red and yellow – it was a nice outfit, actually. But the shoes were all wrong. The woman in the picture was wearing white sneakers and strange red gloves that went up to her elbow. Red gloves? Marion took a closer look.

"Oh my God!" she said out loud. "That's Debbie!" She looked at the next photo and the next. There were close-ups of Debbie's made-up face. She recognized the color of her own lipstick and eyeshadow. She saw the picture of Debbie standing on the metal tracks in the high heeled red sandals.

"Tracks! Oh my God, where is that?! And who took these?!" Marion's surprise turned to worry and even anger as she looked at photo after photo of the Freedom Tunnel. She came upon the photo of Mr. Kaminski, sitting in his office with his arm around Basti.

"Who is that man?!" she almost screamed. Just then Marion heard the front door slam shut.

"Hi, Mom, I'm home!" shouted Debbie from the hall.

"Debbie! Come here right now. Young lady, you have some explaining to do. Who is this man, and where in God's name did you take these photos? I want to know everything. And I mean everything!"

☆

"OK, let's go."

They walked back, sometimes balancing on the shiny metal tracks.

"I wish we would meet him on his way to the office," said Zoe. "I'd like to see how he gets there."

"That's funny, I was just thinking exactly the same thing."

The morning sun broke through the tunnel's gloomy darkness.

"*Hey Basti,*" said Zoe suddenly.

"*Was*?" said Basti.

"*Irgendwie mag ich Mr. Kaminski. Erinnert er dich auch an Opa*?"

"Ja, ein bisschen," said Basti. "But Opa is dead."

"So what, we can still think about him."

Basti then knew what he was going to write on that small area of the Freedom Tunnel wall which he had seen on the last trip. It was deeper into the tunnel than Rick's Borg-man painting, but on the same side. He felt the cans of paint through Rick's black bag. There was white for the background, black and dark blue for the words. Basti had also taken a can of yellow paint. They reached the place. Light came down from above and washed the wall in brightness.

Basti took out his paints and set them on the ground in front of the wall. He first picked up the white, shook it for over a minute, then ten more times for good luck. As Rick had shown him, he started the spray away from the wall. Then he covered the area in white. Next he shook both the black and blue cans of spray paint. He wrote the letters in his mind over and over, while waiting for the white background to dry.

"OK, here we go." Basti squatted down low, bending his knees a bit the way he had seen Rick do. "Get in a groove," Rick had said. "Imagine there is music in your head." Basti began the spray off to the side, then aimed at the wall. That way there wouldn't be a heavy spot of paint at the beginning of the word. The black paint can wrote the first letter: "T". He released his finger from the top, took a deep breath and made the next: "H". And the next: "E". He laughed – he, too, was leaving his mark. He picked up the blue paint and started the next word. A small spray off to the side, then he directed the color onto the wall. Soon a "P" appeared, then "R", "O", "F", "E", "S", "S", "O", and "R".

"Good work, man!" said Basti to himself. "Now, the last word." He put down the blue paint can and picked up the black again. He gave it a good shake, cleaned the tip with his shirt and began.

"L" appeared, then "I", "V", "E" and finally "S !"

Basti stepped back to better see his work. The words just fit into the light. He turned to look at Zoe. She was pointing to her watch.

"How many minutes do we have left?" asked Basti.

"Just seven more," she answered.

"OK, OK, I've just got one more thing to do. I think I can make it in time. You go and find a good place to stand. Just get away from the tracks." Basti pulled out the yellow paint from the bag. He shook it, made a little spray off to the right and then began to paint lines of yellow bursting out from the words, "The Professor Lives!"

"Ba-a-a-s-t-i-i-i!" yelled Zoe. "The train is coming!" He looked to the left and sure enough he could see a sharp light deep in the tunnel's darkness. It was coming closer. He jumped away from the tracks and crouched down, turning his whole body into the dirt-smelling wall. The train rattled by and sounded its horn.

"I'll never get used to that sound," he said to himself, feeling the blood pumping in his ears and in his chest.

When the train had left the tunnel, Zoe and Basti came out from their hiding places.

"I'm still alive!" Basti shouted over to Zoe. Zoe shook her head at her brother's craziness and then looked at his finished work.

"Looks great!" said Zoe. "When did you learn to do that?"

"I got a few lessons from Rick."

"Wow! I'm impressed!" Zoe took out her camera and took a picture. "OK, Picasso, I want to get a shot with you in it. Get over there!"

"Hey, that's no way to talk to a famous artist!" Zoe took a few more photos.

"Time to go, bro," said Basti.

"Yeah, bro, let's go!" said Zoe.

They flew out of the tunnel, screaming at the top of their lungs like two freed birds.

Vocabulary

A

about to do sth. im Begriff sein, etw. zu tun
admit zugeben
aim (n + v) Ziel; zielen
Amtrak amerikanische Eisenbahnlinie
arch Bogen
arrow Pfeil
ashamed beschämt

B

backpack (AE) Rucksack
baggage claim Gepäckausgabe
be sorry leid tun; traurig sein
behave oneself sich benehmen
besides außerdem
bet (n + v) Wette; wetten
bleed bluten
board Tafel; Brett
brain Gehirn
breathe atmen
brick Ziegelstein
bug *ugs.* Insekt, Käfer
bump into s.o. zufällig jdn. treffen
bumper car Autoscooter
burn to death verbrennen

C

can Dose
catchy ansteckend
celebrate feiern
chest Brust
chopsticks Stäbchen
concrete Beton
confused verwirrt
convince überzeugen
cotton candy Zuckerwatte
cough (n + v) Husten; husten
covered bedeckt, übersät
crown Krone
crunchy knusprig
curious neugierig
customs Zoll

D

deep tief
defense Verteidigung
destination Ziel, Richtung
destroy zerstören
dig (up), dug, dug (aus)graben
disappoint enttäuschen
discreet unauffällig
diver Taucher/in
dizzy schwindelig
double-lane zweispurig
dry (v + adj) trocknen; trocken
dust Staub

E

eagle Adler
edge Rand
... (n)either ... auch nicht
embarrassed verlegen
entrance Eingang
entry Eingang
escalator Rolltreppe
especially besonders, insbesondere

every 40 minutes alle 40 Minuten
exasperated genervt
exit Ausgang, Ausfahrt
expense; at Zoe's ~ auf Zoes Kosten
experience (n + v) Erfahrung, Erlebnis; erfahren, erleben
eyebrows; lift one's ~ die Augenbrauen hochziehen

F

fair Kirmes
familiar vertraut, bekannt
fan oneself sich Luft zufächeln
fashion shoot Modeaufnahmen
fence Zaun
figure out herausfinden
firm fest
flashlight Taschenlampe
forearm Unterarm
former der/die/das frühere
foundation Fundament
frame (n + v) Rahmen; rahmen
freed freigelassen
freedom Freiheit
further weiter

G

garbage Müll
gate Tor
ghost Geist
glad froh
glove Handschuh
gravel Schotter
greeting Gruß
guide Reiseführer/in
gym Turnhalle

H

hardly kaum
heavy schwer
heel Ferse, Absatz (am Schuh)
height Höhe
help but nicht umhin können
homeless (n + adj) Obdachlose/r; obdachlos
honest ehrlich
honored geehrt
hopefully hoffentlich
horn Hupe, Signalhorn
hug (n + v) Umarmung; umarmen

I

I'm starved! *ugs.* Ich bin am Verhungern.
impatient ungeduldig
impressed beeindruckt
ink Tinte
insist on sth. auf etw. bestehen
introduce oneself sich vorstellen

L

ladder Leiter
lead (led, led) führen
less weniger
lie (n + v) Lüge; lügen
little wenig
lobby (großer) Eingangsbereich
local train Nahverkehrszug, Vorortszug
low niedrig; tief
lower (v + adj) (ab)senken; untere/r
luggage Gepäck

M

We made it. Wir haben es geschafft.
make a mental note sich etwas merken
make sth. up sich etw. ausdenken, erfinden
marble Marmor
mean gemein; **plain ~** einfach ~
meanwhile inzwischen
memorial Denkmal
mind: in his mind in seinem Kopf, in seinen Gedanken
muss sth. up etw. zersausen
mustache (Oberlippen-)Bart

N

neck Hals
neighborhood Gegend, Nachbarschaft
neither … nor … weder … noch …
Never mind. Egal./ Nicht so wichtig.
notice bemerken

O

observation deck Aussichtsplattform
order (v) bestellen
owner Besitzer/in
oxygen; a bubble of ~ Sauerstoff, ~blase

P

pale blass
parachute Fallschirm
passion Leidenschaft
passport Pass
peace Frieden
post *hier*: Pfosten, Pfahl
pretend so tun als ob
prisoner Gefangene/r
property Eigentum

R

railing Geländer
ray Strahl
reach erreichen
realize bemerken, sich bewusst werden
rear hinter-
recognize wiedererkennen
regards Grüße
relationship Beziehung
relic Rest, Überbleibsel
relief Erleichterung
remind an etw./jdn. erinnern
rent Miete
replace ersetzen
responsibility Verantwortung
retired pensioniert, in Rente
risk (n + v) Risiko; riskieren
roof Dach, Decke
room Raum, Zimmer; Platz
rough rau
rusty rostig

S

scratch kratzen
a few screws loose *ugs.* 'ne Schraube locker
secret (n + adj) Geheimnis; geheim, heimlich
serious ernst, ernsthaft
several einige, etliche
shade Schatten

shake (shook, shaken) schütteln, wackeln
shape (n + v) Form; formen
shoot schießen (auch Fotos); a photo shoot
shore Küste, Land
shot dead erschossen
shrug one's shoulders mit den Schultern zucken
sigh (n + v) Seufzer; seufzen
signature Unterschrift
silk Seide
since seit
sip Schluck
site Baustelle
sketchbook Zeichen-/Skizzenblock
sleeve Ärmel
slice Stück (Pizza, Kuchen etc.)
slightly annoyed leicht genervt
smell (n + v) Geruch; riechen
smoked geräuchert
sneeze niesen
spiderweb Spinnennetz
spread out ausbreiten
squint blinzeln (in der Sonne)
stack Stapel
staircase Treppenaufgang
still (immer) noch; trotzdem
storage room Lagerraum
surface Oberfläche
suspicious verdächtig
swallow (ver-)schlucken

T

take a few days off work ein paar Tage freinehmen
take care (of) aufpassen (auf)
target Ziel
(a game of) 'telephone' Stille Post spielen
thick dick
thin dünn
threaten (be-)drohen
tickle kitzeln
tie down festbinden
tile Fliese
tissue Papiertaschentuch
too bad schade
top hat Zylinder
towel Handtuch
trace Spur
track Gleis
tray Tablett
treasure Schatz
truth Wahrheit

U

ugly hässlich
underwear Unterwäsche
I'm up for it. Ich bin dabei.
upside down umgedreht, auf dem Kopf
get used to sich gewöhnen
I used to go there früher ging ich immer dort hin

V

violate missachten, verletzen

W

wet nass
whatever was (auch) immer
wide breit, weit
wink (n + v) Augenzwinkern; zwinkern
wire Draht
wish wünschen
wrist Handgelenk

Reading tasks

Chapter 1

1. Zoe and Basti's dad has a short talk with both kids on the night before they leave. What does Zoe remember about this conversation? What does Basti remember?
2. Make a list of five situations that might be dangerous in a big city.
3. How did you learn about about what happened in New York on September 11, 2001?

Chapter 2

1. There is graffiti all over the world. What is graffiti? What do you think are the different reasons why people make it – or hate it?
2. Have you ever seen street stickers in your town? What are the differences between street stickers and graffiti?
3. Do you think the trip up to the top of the Empire State Building is worth the ticket price? Or is a 'virtual tour' on the Internet just as good?

Chapter 3

1. If Rick described the Freedom Tunnel to you, would you be interested in going? What would you do there?
2. Do you think the kids were careful enough down in the Freedom Tunnel? How could they have made it a safer trip?
3. Why do Rick, Basti and Zoe leave the tunnel before Rick's friends do?

Chapter 4

1. Describe Rick and Debbie's relationship.
2. Imagine you are Debbie and you have just listened to the other kids' story about the tunnel. Would you be curious to go?
3. Rick and Debbie have different plans for the next day. How do they decide what to do?
4. What is Coney Island like? What do the kids do there?
5. Coney Island has a long history as the 'amusement park' for New Yorkers. Look up Coney Island on the Internet. Present what you have found in your class.

Chapter 5

1. Describe the reason of each of the four cousins for going to the Freedom Tunnel. Is what they are going to do dangerous?
2. Are there any places near you which might be good locations for a photo shoot? Or for a wall painting, a theater performance or even a special kind of party? Describe the place.

Chapter 6

1. What Penn Station 'artefacts' does Mr. Kaminski describe? Why do you think he is telling Basti all this?
2. What makes Mr. Kaminski remember stories about his past?

Chapter 7

1. Why does Basti think it really strange when he and Zoe meet Moog on Brooklyn Bridge?
2. Who lived in the Lower East Side when Mr. Kaminski was a boy? What was this neighborhood like back then?

3. What's wrong with Rick when he arrives at the Chinese restaurant?

Chapter 8

1. Do you think it was a mistake for Rick to go to the ghost station?
2. Re-read your list of dangerous situations that you wrote after reading the first chapter. Have you changed your mind about some of them? Would you write a different list now?
3. If there were no trains running through the Freedom Tunnel, what do you think would be the best way to use the empty tunnel?

Chapter 9

1. Describe the people Basti meets at Penn Station.
2. Draw a comic strip of Basti's trip to Penn Station and to the security guard's office. Don't forget to include the big lady behind the baggage claim counter!

Chapter 10

1. Why is Aunt Marion so angry when she sees the photos? What do you think will happen when Zoe and Basti come home?
2. When she returns to Germany, Zoe wants to post her photographs on a website for 'Urban Explorers'. Write a short paragraph for Zoe describting her tunnel experience.

A note on the author

Cecile Rossant was born in New York City, where she went to school and university. She worked as an architect in New York and Tokyo and then came to Berlin in 1995 where she now lives with her husband and two children.

Even though she left New York years ago, it's always in her imagination. "I rode the subway to school every day and was always curious about the dark tunnels beyond the station. Finally, in high school, with a few good friends, I entered that dark, exciting world and had an adventure I'll never forget."

Cecile Rossant is also the author of a novel, *Tokyo Bay Traffic,* and a collection of short stories, *About Face*.